NEW DIRECTIONS FOR TEACHING AND LEARNING

Marilla D. Svinicki, *University of Texas, Austin*
EDITOR-IN-CHIEF

R. Eugene Rice, *American Association for Higher Education*
CONSULTING EDITOR

The Importance of Physical Space in Creating Supportive Learning Environments

Nancy Van Note Chism
Indiana University–Purdue University Indianapolis

Deborah J. Bickford
University of Dayton

EDITORS

◕ **W9-ASH-825**

Number 92, Winter 2002

JOSSEY-BASS
San Francisco

THE IMPORTANCE OF PHYSICAL SPACE IN CREATING SUPPORTIVE LEARNING
ENVIRONMENTS
Nancy Van Note Chism, Deborah J. Bickford (eds.)
New Directions for Teaching and Learning, no. 92
Marilla D. Svinicki, Editor-in-Chief
R. Eugene Rice, Consulting Editor

Microfilm copies of issues and articles are available in 16mm and 35mm,
as well as microfiche in 105mm, through University Microfilms Inc., 300
North Zeeb Road, Ann Arbor, Michigan 48106-1346.

ISSN 0271-0633   electronic ISSN 1536-0768

NEW DIRECTIONS FOR TEACHING AND LEARNING is part of The Jossey-Bass
Higher and Adult Education Series and is published quarterly by Wiley
Subscription Services, Inc., A Wiley Company, at Jossey-Bass, 989 Market Street, San Francisco, California 94103-1741. Periodicals postage paid
at San Francisco, California, and at additional mailing offices. Postmas-
ter: Send address changes to New Directions for Teaching and Learning,
Jossey-Bass, 989 Market Street, San Francisco, California 94103-1741.

New Directions for Teaching and Learning is indexed in College Student
Personnel Abstracts, Contents Pages in Education, and Current Index to
Journals in Education (ERIC).

SUBSCRIPTIONS cost $70.00 for individuals and $145 for institutions, agen-
cies, and libraries. Prices subject to change.

EDITORIAL CORRESPONDENCE should be sent to the editor-in-chief, Marilla
D. Svinicki, The Center for Teaching Effectiveness, University of Texas at
Austin, Main Building 2200, Austin, TX 78712-1111.

Cover photograph by Richard Blair/Color & Light © 1990.

www.josseybass.com

Printed in the United States of America on acid-free recycled paper containing at least 20 percent postconsumer wase.

CONTENTS

About This Publication. Since 1980, *New Directions for Teaching and Learning (NDTL)* has brought a unique blend of theory, research, and practice to leaders in postsecondary education. *NDTL* volumes strive not only for solid substance but also for timeliness, compactness, and accessibility.

The series has four goals: to inform readers about current and future directions in teaching and learning in postsecondary education, to illuminate the context that shapes these new directions, to illustrate these new directions through examples from real settings, and to propose ways in which these new directions can be incorporated into still other settings.

This publication reflects the view that teaching deserves respect as a high form of scholarship. We believe that significant scholarship is conducted not only by researchers who report results of empirical investigations but also by practitioners who share disciplined reflections about teaching. Contributors to *NDTL* approach questions of teaching and learning as seriously as they approach substantive questions in their own disciplines, and they deal not only with pedagogical issues but also with the intellectual and social context in which these issues arise. Authors deal on one hand with theory and research and on the other with practice, and they translate from research and theory to practice and back again.

About This Volume. Many institutions today have embraced the new paradigms for learning that involve interaction and change, only to find that the old paradigms for space design defeat their efforts. As a result they are thinking about ways to redesign their campuses to accommodate these new ideas. This issue speaks to both the process and outcomes that result when campus teams set out on the path of producing new learning spaces.

Marilla D. Svinicki
Editor-in-Chief

MARILLA D. SVINICKI *is director of the Center for Teaching Effectiveness at the University of Texas at Austin.*

Editors' Notes

According to Banning and Canard (1986), "Among the many methods employed to foster student development, the use of the physical environment is perhaps the least understood and the most neglected." Faculty and students alike have become so accustomed to meeting in spaces that are sterile in appearance, unable to accommodate different instructional approaches, and uncomfortable for supporting adult bodies that most have taken these conditions as a fact of college life. The lack of extensive dialogue on the importance of learning spaces in higher education environments prompted the production of this volume.

The chapter authors look at the topic of learning spaces from a variety of perspectives, elaborating on the relationship between physical space and learning, arguing for an expanded notion of the concept of learning spaces and furnishings, talking about the context within which decision making for learning spaces takes place, and discussing promising approaches to the renovation of old learning spaces and the construction of new ones.

The volume begins with foundation in theory. In Chapter One, Nancy Van Note Chism offers an overview of the literature in the field, then focuses on the connections that have been made between modern learning theory and learning spaces. Ken Graetz and Michael Goliber use Chapter Two to provide background on what is known about how humans respond to space. Working within the modern context of collaborative learning and information technology, they detail implications for space design, primarily from the field of environmental psychology, the study of the relationship between people and their physical environment.

The next two chapters deal with expanding understanding of the definitions of learning spaces and furniture. In Chapter Three, Thomas Skill and Brian Young discuss the concept of learning spaces. They draw on popular principles of effective practice to talk about their implications for spaces that can serve the needs of students in face-to-face as well as virtual environments. Paul Cornell talks about the essential role of furniture in Chapter Four, portraying the ways in which furniture is at the heart of the flexibility needed to "decenter" classrooms, create learning environments in nonclassroom spaces, move from one mode of interaction to another, enable collaboration, accommodate technology, and be suitable to learners of different ages and needing different physical accommodations.

We wish to recognize the contribution of Melody Cook Coryell, administrative specialist at Indiana University–Purdue University Indianapolis, who checked references, standardized style, and deftly performed other necessary tasks involved in the production of this volume.

1

The planning process, another important dimension of the issue of learning spaces, is next treated. An in-depth look at the planning and implementation processes for creating learning environments is the topic of Chapter Five. Deborah Bickford focuses on the present process at most campuses, exploring how politics, finances, standards, and other features routinely interact, proposing a new vision for how planning can work more effectively and collaboratively. In Chapter Six, James Butz speaks from the perspectives of architect and educational facilities consultant on how educators can make best use of partnerships with architects.

The volume next turns to examples of good planning and implementation processes. A model planning process used at the University of Guelph is at the heart of a case study by Julia Christensen Hughes in Chapter Seven. Beginning with a planning approach that surveyed faculty and students on classroom design and learning technology preferences and also included the voices of others with a stake in learning spaces, the planning process identified the main factors that were important, such as capacity to accommodate different pedagogies, and key operational issues, such as a comprehensive classroom management system. In Chapter Eight, Joan DeGuire North details a case study of a campus that approached the renovation of existing spaces with new learning theory in mind. The chapter describes how simple strategies made the task of converting old spaces more economically feasible as well as how new issues and problems arise when learning spaces become more flexible.

Adding to the repertoire of cases, William Dittoe in Chapter Nine provides an overview of innovative models of new and renovated learning environments from campuses around the country. The descriptive text explains why these spaces are important to the educational process and how they relate to the concepts articulated in the preceding chapters.

Chapter Ten summarizes the main arguments. Coeditors Nancy Van Note Chism and Deborah Bickford provide a summary of the major ideas and implications discussed in this volume and pose a series of critical considerations regarding learning environments.

We have augmented this volume with a Web site (http://spacesforlearning.udayton.edu) to house all the Web references that authors have used in the text, so that the currency of the original references can be maintained. The Web site also contains diagrams, virtual tours, additional documents pertaining to learning space design, and links to other relevant sites. This site also has an interactional dimension so that the conversation will continue. The background readings here are intended to stimulate a conversation that has been too limited in the past—a conversation that should be more visionary and more inclusive as it explores and seeks to improve the physical environments that wield such influence over learning in higher education.

Nancy Van Note Chism
Deborah J. Bickford
Editors

Reference

Banning, J. H., and Canard, M. R. "The Physical Environment Supports Student Development." *Campus Ecologist*, 1986, 4(1). [http://spacesforlearning.udayton.edu].

NANCY VAN NOTE CHISM *is associate dean of the faculties and associate vice chancellor for professional development at Indiana University–Purdue University Indianapolis, and associate professor of higher education and student affairs at Indiana University.*

DEBORAH J. BICKFORD *is associate provost for learning, learning environments, and pedagogy, co-director of the Learning Village, and associate professor of management at the University of Dayton.*

1

We know too much about how learning occurs to continue to ignore the ways in which learning spaces are planned, constructed, and maintained.

A Tale of Two Classrooms

Nancy Van Note Chism

From the instructor's station at the front of 313 Fulton Hall, the view would be comical if it weren't so frustrating. Looking out on this undergraduate class in information science, the instructor sees the backs of forty computer monitors facing him, rather than the human beings that they hide. One wonders if the cyborgs have arrived. At the front of the room, the technology is wonderful—a speedy machine, a nice large display screen. There is very little surface for the instructor's materials, so he has piled his notes and books on a chair.

The instructor begins class with a greeting and takes attendance by walking up and down the center aisle, which affords him a sidewise row-by-row view of the students sitting at the monitors. He then provides an overview of the main concepts he wants students to work with and uses presentation software to display a nice outline. While he talks, he tries to connect with students, but since his view is quite obstructed, he once again takes to walking up and down the aisle, having to return periodically to advance the slides. Some students are paying attention and taking notes; others are surfing the Web or doing e-mail, unable to resist the distraction before them.

A proponent of active learning, the instructor next has an exercise that he would like the students to do in pairs. He posts the activity on the screen, gives very clear directions, and begins to circulate as the students work. It is easy enough for the students to pull chairs together to work on one computer for each pair, and they become engrossed in the exercise, which involves evaluating Web sites. As the instructor walks around, he can talk with the groups closest to the center aisle, but those who have chosen to sit toward the walls on either side are not within his range. It is clear that the only collaborative computing work he can assign must involve pairs since

NEW DIRECTIONS FOR TEACHING AND LEARNING, no. 92, Winter 2002 © Wiley Periodicals, Inc.

students would not be able to pull more than two chairs together to see the monitors, which are set in rows.

At the end of the time for the activity, the instructor wants each group to talk about what they found, but this exchange is difficult to conduct because students cannot see each other over the monitors and the depth of the room makes it hard to hear comments across the distance. The instructor continually has to prompt students to speak more loudly. Several students begin to tune out and revert to individually surfing the Web or doing e-mail. Valiantly, the instructor sums up the main outcomes of the lesson and dismisses the class as the time draws to an end.

Meanwhile, in 014 College Tower, a second instructor is also conducting a class designed in several components. This class is for graduate students studying research methods. The room that has been assigned to this class has six round tables, each with six chairs. There is a video monitor and VCR on a cart in one corner, an overhead projector on another cart, and an instructor's table at the front of the room. It seems that the room might have been originally set up for students preparing to be elementary teachers, as permanent lines designed to accommodate handwriting instruction are affixed to the chalkboard. Inspired by the lines, the instructor jokingly writes the name of a reference on the board in exaggerated "Perfect Palmer Method" handwriting as the students assemble.

This instructor also begins class with a greeting and an overview of the session topic. Since the students are sitting at round tables, some must rotate their chairs or crane their necks to see the front of the room, and the instructor tries to accommodate the multiple viewing angles by walking around as she talks. As she uses overhead transparencies, she attempts to control the lighting so that there is good contrast, but the lights cannot be controlled by zone, so she apologizes for there being too much light around the screen for good visibility.

Like her colleague, this instructor also wants students to work in groups and she outlines the task. Students begin to work together, talking easily and with animation. It is clear that they know each other and are comfortable working together. The room becomes quite noisy, but students accommodate to the environment by leaning in toward their group members to hear. The instructor, in designing group tasks for this class, realizes that she has to think in terms of six groups of six. Once, when she really needed groups of four, she sent two groups to the library to work.

When it is time for this class to talk together, their being seated at round tables creates the problem of having to arch around to see the speaker, but they do so without great effort, and the class concludes.

The Influence of Design

As classrooms go, these rooms are probably not the subjects of many complaints. They are modern, clean, and well equipped. The climate control is not a problem, and the furniture is in good condition. Instructors and students alike routinely make accommodations to accomplish their work in these rooms, often with humor and creativity. For the most part, they do not think about the ways in which these rooms are shaping their interactions—and their learning. When we isolate the rooms for examination from this perspective, however, it is clear that room design influences the social context of the classes, student-instructor and student-student relations, instructional design options, and the overall effectiveness of instructional technology.

In both cases, the instructors were assigned to rooms that were designed for a specific purpose—one a computer lab and the other a resource room for education students. Flexibility was clearly not a top consideration. The person presently doing room scheduling either had no other space or did not realize that the rooms were unsuitable for the kinds of instruction taking place, basing the decision on limited information such as class enrollments and locations of the department offices of the instructors. Were the rooms designed as general issue classrooms, however, the problems with flexibility might still remain, since often so-called all-purpose rooms have fixed seating, a clear front and back that favors teacher talk and projection rather than class participation, and space capacity limitations that prevent movement and reorientation.

The room designs of Fulton 313 and 014 College Tower during original construction were probably constrained by the tight economic situation that exists at most campuses, with zoned lighting, recessed monitors, and extra space ruled out for their costliness. Because the rooms are in an institution with a classroom shortage and are less than ten years old, they will probably remain the way they are and continue to be assigned to multiple kinds of classes for some time to come.

Low levels of awareness on how learning spaces influence learning outcomes, coupled with the complexities involved in building and maintaining learning spaces, have kept the topic of learning spaces from emerging for extensive public discussion. While a select few individuals on most campuses—the architect, the facilities maintenance director, the budget officer, and perhaps the registrar and technology director—have been involved in learning space design issues, it has been less traditional for the users—the faculty and the students—to play any significant role in this arena. Although they occasionally grumble, particularly when classrooms are shabby, too hot, or too cold, users of academic spaces often take the limitations of the physical environment for granted and do not demand involvement. Planners usually assume that the expertise needed to design spaces is technical in nature and that the constraints of funding narrow the choices available to the extent that input from users would not be productive or efficient.

Insights from the Literature

A search for literature on the topic of learning spaces reveals a variety of approaches:

- *Basic research about space, place, perception, and learning from several disciplinary perspectives.* These pieces discuss such topics as how memory is associated with place; how crowding, temperature, noise, physical discomfort, and other factors affect performance; and how physical proximity influences communication. An example is Gallagher's *The Power of Place* (1994).

- *Writing that applies theoretical perspectives from some of these areas to the issue of learning spaces.* Very few pieces fall into this category and most of the literature is dated. An exception is the chapter on physical environments in Strange and Banning's *Educating by Design* (2001). Previously, Griffin (1990) had summarized much of the then-available literature in a field often labeled *classroom ecology.* The physical space dimensions of this issue are the topic of occasional pieces in the *Campus Ecologist,* available through the Web site for this volume at http://spacesforlearning.udayton.edu. Interestingly, some firms dealing in classroom design or furnishings have synthesized the literature and applied it in their newsletters and occasional papers series. For an example, see Steelcase's "Learning Environments for the Information Age" (also accessible through the volume's Web site). Chapter Two of this volume elaborates on the approach of ecological psychology to learning environments.

- *Design specification literature that usually focuses on instructional technology.* Many institutions have specifications for classrooms or computer labs on the World Wide Web. They usually describe technical requirements for conduit, height of projection screens, lighting controls, equipment rack placement, and the like. Rarely is there any mention in these specifications of the different purposes that learning spaces need to accommodate. The assumption is that there will be presentational material that students will view, that the teacher's voice needs to be heard, and that the students need sight lines but not voice amplification (because they will *not* need to be heard). An exception is Daniel Niemeyer from the University of Colorado, whose extensive Web site discusses pedagogical considerations as well as design specifications. Niemeyer's site can be accessed through http://spaces forlearning.udayton.edu.

- *Descriptions of innovative learning spaces.* This is not an extensive literature, but some overviews of learning spaces, complete with photographs or diagrams, appear in the literature and on the Web. An example is Jack Wilson's "The Development of the Studio Classroom," a piece on an instructional and physical space innovation at Rensselaer Polytechnic Institute (access available at http://spacesforlearning.udayton.edu). Chapter Nine of this volume illustrates some additional spaces.

- *Research on the impact of different physical arrangements for learning.* The literature on this aspect of learning spaces is even sparser. Most of the pieces concentrate on elementary school settings. An example is Sommer and Olsen's work (1980), which summarizes the differences observed in participation rates and student-student interactions in straight-row versus seminar-style classroom arrangements.

• *Discussions of the planning process and visions for the future.* Foremost among these are discussions of cyberspace or the community as the new learning environment, as in Roger Schank's provocative "Death of the Classroom" ideas (Fielding, 1999).

What Learning Theory Implies for Space

An important foundational issue underlies consideration of any approach to the issue of learning spaces: What kind of learning are we striving to promote in colleges and universities and how does space influence our ability to do so? Indeed, advances in cognitive psychology and responsive innovations in pedagogy have challenged the adequacy of traditional learning spaces. When the "transmission" theory of learning dominated, inspiring the corresponding pedagogy of "teaching as telling," rooms that were configured for a teacher to be seen and heard and for students to take notes were the norm. Hebdige (1979) described the classic arrangement: "The hierarchical relationship between teacher and taught is inscribed in the very layout of the lecture theatre where the seating arrangements—benches rising in tiers before a raised lectern—dictate the flow of information and serve to 'naturalize' professorial authority. Thus, a whole range of decisions about what is and what is not possible within education have been made, however unconsciously, before the content of the individual courses is even decided (pp. 12–13)."

In the last twenty years, however, higher education has seen a variety of challenges to the transmission theory. These have come from cognitive theorists, who have focused on the ways in which human beings construct new knowledge and on the ways in which the social context influences learning; anthropologists, sociologists, and cultural theorists, who have questioned our assumptions about the nature of knowledge; and neuroscientists and evolutionary biologists, who have studied the physical processes involved in learning. Several contemporary summaries of these advances and their impact on higher education thought are available. (See the resource list at the end of this chapter.)

While a rich array of propositions are being explored and argued across these fields, it is clear that consensus on a number of ideas is at the heart of the discussion. Ten of these principles were enumerated by a task force convened by the American Association for Higher Education, American College Personnel Association, and National Association of Student Personnel Administrators through their joint project, *Powerful Partnerships: A Shared Responsibility for Learning.* Known as "Learning Principles and Collaborative Action" (1998), these principles summarize findings of modern theorists and derive implications for practice. Briefly, the ten principles claim that learning

• Is about making and maintaining connections
• Takes place in the context of a compelling situation

- Is an active search for meaning by the learner
- Is developmental and involves the whole person
- Is done by individuals within a social context
- Is affected by the educational climate *(this principle is particularly relevant for this volume since it calls attention to settings and surroundings)*
- Requires frequent feedback
- Takes place informally and incidentally
- Is grounded in particular contexts and individual experiences
- Involves the ability of individuals to monitor their own learning

In this new constructivist thinking, where teachers serve as facilitators for active student engagement, where learning occurs in many locations, and where power is distributed across actors, learning space needs are seen to be far more dynamic and situational than they were under the transmission model. The new way of thinking about facilitating learning implies the need for small-group meeting spaces, project spaces, spaces for whole-class dialogue where the students as well as the teacher can be seen and heard, spaces where technology can be accessed easily, spaces for display of ideas and working documents, and spaces that can accommodate movement and noise. What's more, the spaces are likely not all to be in traditional academic classrooms. Spillover spaces in wide corridors or lobbies outside classrooms, outdoor spaces, and spaces that include possibilities for food and Internet access are all needed. Of course, there is also cyberspace, a learning space we have yet to think about as space. (See Chapter Three of this volume for an expanded discussion of this issue.)

The capacity for space to influence motivation and establish a social culture, two concepts that clearly are key in modern learning theory, is also receiving wider recognition. Advances in ergonomics, design of corporate spaces, and new thinking about home design have all highlighted the ways in which comfort and aesthetics influence performance. Classroom furniture manufacturers have begun to introduce new lines of products. No longer assuming the traditional power differential between teacher and student nor expecting that the new student can be satisfied by a cramped and uncomfortable tablet-arm chair, these manufacturers have been producing alternative types of seating more suitable to adult learners. (Chapter Four of this volume treats the topic of furniture in more depth.)

Lighting and acoustics designers have taken on the challenge of learning spaces, proposing arrangements that allow for variation in the location of the focus of the action and use of technology. Designers attuned to the influence of the motivational dimensions of learning spaces are beginning to point out that wall and floor surfaces in learning spaces need to be pleasing to the eye as well as functional. And others are beginning to lobby for more art and decorative pieces that are instructional in themselves in lieu of the tattered map or periodic chart of the elements that often constitutes the main decorative element of a learning space.

These changes are prompted by market forces as well as by changes in teaching approaches: the competition for students among colleges and universities and between these institutions and the corporate world is at an all-time high. At the same time, the financial picture at most institutions of higher education is bleak, resulting in further cuts to already constrained construction and renovation budgets. A radical rethinking of the use of space in learning, exploring related items such as scheduling and the use of instructional technology, is clearly needed at this juncture. As with many challenges, this need to rethink space issues can suggest opportunities and new ways of operating, courses of action that will be responsive to the ways in which contemporary scholars suggest learning can best be facilitated.

References

American Association for Higher Education, American College Personnel Association, and National Association of Student Personnel Administrators. "Learning Principles and Collaborative Action." Excerpted from *Powerful Partnerships: A Shared Responsibility for Learning,* 1998. [http://spacesforlearning.udayton.edu].

Banning, J. H. (ed.). "Campus Ecologist." Fort Collins, Colo.: Carolyn Banning, n.d. [http://spacesforlearning.udayton.edu].

Fielding, R. "The Death of the Classroom: Learning Cycles and Roger Schank," 1999. [http://spacesforlearning.udayton.edu].

Gallagher, W. *The Power of Place: How Our Surroundings Shape Our Thoughts, Emotions, and Actions.* New York: Harper Perennial Library, 1994 (originally published 1993).

Griffin, T. "The Physical Environment of the College Classroom and Its Effects on Students." *Campus Ecologist,* 1990, 8(1). [http://spacesforlearning.udayton.edu].

Hebdige, D. *Subculture: The Meaning of Style.* London: Methuen, 1979.

Niemeyer, D. "Classroom Design Principles That Improve Teaching and Learning," n.d. [http://spacesforlearning.udayton.edu].

Sommer, R., and Olsen, H. "The Soft Classroom." *Environment and Behavior,* 1980, 12(1), 3–16.

Steelcase Corporation. "Learning Environments for the Information Age," 2000. [http://spacesforlearning.udayton.edu].

Strange, C. C., and Banning, J. H. (eds.). *Educating by Design: Creating Campus Learning Environments That Work.* San Francisco: Jossey-Bass, 2001.

Wilson, J. M. "The Development of the Studio Classroom," n.d. [http://spacesfor learning.udayton.edu].

Other Resources on Learning in Higher Education

Bruning, R. H. "The College Classroom from the Perspective of Cognitive Psychology." In K. W. Pritchard and R. M. Sawyer (eds.), *Handbook of College Teaching.* Westport, Conn.: Greenwood, 1994.

Cassaza, M. E., and Silverman, S. L. *Learning Assistance and Developmental Education.* San Francisco: Jossey-Bass, 1996.

Committee on the Foundations of Assessment, J. Pellegrino, N. Chudowsky, and R. Glaser (eds.). *Knowing What Students Know: The Science and Design of Educational Assessment.* Washington, D.C.: Center for Education, National Research Council, 2001.

Jarvis, P., Holford, J., and Griffin, C. *The Theory and Practice of Learning.* London: Kogan Page, 1998.

Marchese, T. J. "The New Conversations About Learning: Insights from Neuroscience and Anthropology, Cognitive Science and Work-Place Studies." In B. L. Cambridge (ed.), *Assessing Impact: Evidence and Action*. Washington, D.C.: American Association for Higher Education, 1997. [http://spacesforlearning.udayton.edu].

Merriam, S. B., and Caffarella, R. S. *Learning in Adulthood: A Comprehensive Guide*. (2nd ed.) San Francisco: Jossey-Bass, 1999.

Stage, F. K., Muller, P. A., Kinzie, J., and Simmons, A. *Creating Learner-Centered Classrooms: What Does Learning Theory Have to Say?* ASHE-ERIC Higher Education Report, vol. 26, no. 4. Washington, D.C.: Graduate School of Education and Human Development, George Washington University, 1998.

Svinicki, M. D. "New Directions in Learning and Motivation." In M. D. Svinicki (ed.), *Teaching and Learning at the Edge of the Millennium: Building on What We Have Learned*. New Directions for Teaching and Learning, no. 80. San Francisco: Jossey-Bass, 1999.

Tennant, M., and Pogson, P. *Learning and Change in the Adult Years: A Developmental Perspective*. San Francisco: Jossey-Bass, 1995.

NANCY VAN NOTE CHISM *is associate dean of the faculties and associate vice chancellor for professional development at Indiana University–Purdue University Indianapolis, and associate professor of higher education and student affairs at Indiana University.*

2

Physical environment plays an important role in shaping human social interaction. This chapter explores this issue from a psychological perspective, drawing on theories and research from environmental and social psychology. It explores characteristics of effective collaborative work environments.

Designing Collaborative Learning Places: Psychological Foundations and New Frontiers

Ken A. Graetz, Michael J. Goliber

As an alternative to lecture, imagine engaging your students in a collaborative activity during your next class meeting. You divide the class into five small groups and ask each group to solve a problem and present a solution. Anyone who has attempted such a feat can attest to the inadequacy of most college classrooms for supporting group work and the importance of the physical environment in determining the success of collaborative learning. What would the ideal collaborative learning place look like? Brufee (1999) describes it in these terms: "A level floor, movable seats, chalkboards on three or four walls, controlled acoustics (acoustical-tiled ceilings and carpeted floors), and no central seminar table (or one that can be pushed well out of the way without threatening an attack of lumbago). An alternative is six to ten movable four- or five-sided tables of roughly card-table size" (p. 259).

Although common sense should guide the design of collaborative learning places, the notion that meaningful and efficient collaboration can occur anywhere ignores the important role of the physical environment in shaping human social interaction. This chapter explores the issue from a psychological perspective, drawing on literature from environmental and social psychology. It begins with a discussion of the predicted shift from expository lectures to collaborative activities as the primary function of fixed-site classrooms. Next, three environmental issues are explored: attitudes and place attachment, lighting and temperature, and density and noise. The chapter closes with two specific examples of effective collaborative learning environments, a physical classroom called the Studio and an online collaborative application called Lotus QuickPlace.

NEW DIRECTIONS FOR TEACHING AND LEARNING, no. 92, Winter 2002   © Wiley Periodicals, Inc.

13

Information Technology and Collaborative Learning

Information technology will have a major impact on classroom design over the next decade, one that won't be addressed by simply adding network drops to existing lecture halls. Rapid advances in information technology have set the stage for the migration of expository lecture from the classroom to the network. A growing number of college students already have constant online access to course syllabi, presentations, lecture notes, and other materials. This mode of information delivery improves on previous attempts to lecture at a distance (such as by television) in terms of its ease of access, controllability, and interactivity. Digital course content is becoming richer, deeper, and more interactive with the use of animation, multimedia, and programming languages. An increasing number of studies indicate no significant difference in the amount of factual information learned when comparing traditional lectures with electronic information delivery. Combine this with research dating back a half century indicating that traditional lectures do little to inspire course-related thought or interest and are relatively ineffective for teaching course-related values, behavioral skills, and procedural knowledge (Bligh, 2000), and it appears that lectures are destined for obsolescence.

What impact will the demise of traditional lectures have on classroom design? Although some predict that fixed-site classrooms will no longer be necessary, it is more likely that these spaces will be needed for new purposes (Grauerholtz, McKenzie, and Romero, 1999). It seems reasonable to assume that one of the primary functions of fixed-site classrooms in the near future will be to support discussion, teamwork, and collaboration (Steele and Marshall, 1996). Collaborative learning refers to a wide variety of "educational activities in which human relationships are the key to welfare, achievement, and mastery," wherein teachers "help students learn by working together on substantive issues" (Brufee, 1999, p. 83). Collaborative learning can take many forms, from group discussion to team projects (Adams and Hamm, 1996; Brookfield and Preskill, 1999).

When will the transformation from traditional lecture to collaborative learning occur? Borrowing from Mark Twain, rumors of the death of lectures have been greatly exaggerated. Surveys suggest that the expository lecture is still the most common format used by college educators in the United States (Bligh, 2000). The continued use of lectures should not be blamed entirely on the intransigence of college instructors. It is a good bet that most instructors would rather be doing something else. Their continued use of lectures probably stems from situational factors, specifically, the absence of support for alternative methods (in the form of training and best practices), the absence of extrinsic incentives to change, and the requirement to use classroom facilities inadequate for supporting collaboration. It is the latter restraining force that can be addressed through better classroom design, again raising the question, What would a collaborative learning place look like?

Psychological Foundations

Most of the empirical literature pertaining to the design of educational environments is found in environmental psychology, the study of the relationship between individuals and their physical environment (Gifford, 1997), and social psychology, the study of how people think about, influence, and relate to one another (Myers, 1999). Weinstein's (1981) four assumptions about educational environments provide a valuable point of departure. First is the notion that the physical classroom can facilitate or inhibit learning, both directly (through noise, crowding) and symbolically (as when students attribute poor classroom design and maintenance to lack of respect on the part of the institution). Second, the effects of the physical environment on learning are often moderated by other social, psychological, and instructional variables. Third, the learning environment should match teaching objectives, student learning styles, and, most important, the social setting. Finally, Weinstein argues that learning is optimized only when the physical environment is treated with the same care as curricular materials and teacher preparation.

Although these assumptions underscore the general need to focus on the physical learning environment, more specific recommendations for the design of collaborative learning places are required. Tentative recommendations can be drawn from the existing research on environmental attitudes and place attachment, lighting and temperature, and density and noise. These variables were selected because they appear to have a strong influence on social behavior and may also have an impact on the effectiveness of collaborative learning.

Attitudes and Place Attachment. In psychology, an attitude typically refers to a perceiver's positive or negative evaluation of a target, in this case a physical classroom. As students enter a classroom, they form an impression of that space and experience an associated emotional response. Much of the work in this area has been influenced by Gibson's (1966, 1979) notion of environmental affordances. Gibson suggested that the substances (glass, steel, wood) and surfaces (tables, walls, floors) in a physical environment provide immediate information as to the setting's likely function. Thus desks arranged in rows facing a central podium suggest lecture, whereas tables scattered about the room suggest collaboration.

People's preference for a specific setting appears to depend heavily on their cognitive impression. Kaplan and Kaplan (1982) suggest four cognitive determinants of environmental preference: coherence, or the ease with which a setting can be organized cognitively; complexity, or the perceived capacity of the setting to occupy interest and stimulate activity; legibility, or perceived ease of use, and mystery, or the perception that entering the setting would lead to increased learning, interaction, or interest.

Most college classrooms are highly coherent and legible. They make perfect sense to students who expect to sit quietly and listen to a lecture. The initial complexity and mystery of the typical college classroom probably dissipates quickly over time, leaving an impression of the setting as familiar but boring. This impression is likely to change if the instructor attempts to use the classroom in a manner that does not agree with its affordances. Thus, using a lecture hall to support collaborative activities may lead to a negative emotional response that inhibits collaboration. On the other hand, permanently changing the classroom environment to support collaboration will bring affordances in line with student impressions, resulting in an environment that is both understandable and engaging.

As people live and work in physical settings, they may develop a strong connection to a particular location that goes beyond simple preference. Psychologically, the location changes from a physical space to a place that has profound meaning for the individual (Tuan, 1974). Attachment to specific college learning spaces is a fascinating but virtually unexplored concept. To the great relief of alumni relations directors, many students have a strong place attachment to their college. College planners might do well to consider student and instructor place attachment as a major goal of classroom design. This goal may often be overlooked in an environment where students and instructors are required to move from one classroom to another every fifty minutes and where instructors are often assigned to different classrooms each academic term. Under current conditions, most students and instructors have little opportunity to develop meaningful attachments to classrooms.

Lighting and Temperature. Thanks to fluorescent lights and climate control, classroom lighting and temperature tend to be relatively homogeneous across campuses and are probably not as carefully scrutinized by classroom designers as other features of the learning environment. However, they are the first things that most students notice about a classroom and certainly give rise to complaints when they deviate from comfortable levels. What effects do these variables have on collaborative learning?

Although research suggests that classroom temperature does affect learning (Wyon, 1970), it probably has greater impact on social behavior. Excessive heat is a well-documented environmental irritant that appears to cause hostile thoughts, feelings, and behaviors in some individuals (Anderson, Deuser, and DeNeve, 1995). When working in groups versus watching a traditional lecture, students are often sitting closer to one another and are more active physically. In addition, they may also be gathered around computers and projectors that generate heat. Relative to lecture halls, the average temperature of collaborative classrooms may need to be reduced.

With respect to classroom lighting, an ongoing debate in environmental psychology pertains to the relative merits of full-spectrum or daylight fluorescent lamps versus the more common cool white fluorescent lamp. Although exposure to traditional fluorescent lighting does not appear to affect student health, research indicates that it does produce heightened levels of physiological arousal in students, particularly in those who are already prone to arousal (for example, in hyperactive or autistic individuals; see Coleman, Frankel, Ritvo, and Freeman, 1976). There is also evidence that exposure to traditional fluorescent lighting reduces student sociability (Kuller and Lindsten, 1992). This does not mean that dim incandescent lighting is the best choice for collaborative classrooms. Evidence suggests that dim lighting may lead to a loss of self-awareness and normative inhibition (Prentice-Dunn and Rogers, 1980). Thus the optimal choice for collaborative classrooms may be normal intensity, full-spectrum or daylight fluorescent lighting.

Density and Noise. A considerable amount of research has explored the psychological and educational effects of classroom density, both spatial (that is, the size of the room) and social (that is, the number of students). In their meta-analysis of seventy-seven different studies on this issue, Glass and Smith (1978) concluded that higher social density results in lower student achievement. Interestingly, this relationship was not as pronounced for class sizes of more than twenty students. This may indicate that the effects of density are moderated by classroom activity. When listening to a traditional lecture in a large group, an increase in density may not have a detrimental effect on learning. When engaged in a collaborative activity that requires mobility, high density may be more problematic (Heller, Groff, and Solomon, 1977; Weinstein, 1979). When designing collaborative classrooms, spatial density should be such that both students and instructors have enough room to move easily from group to group (that is, four to seven feet between groups).

Designers should also pay careful attention to the degree to which students feel crowded in a classroom, a psychological state that does not always correspond to actual classroom density. People may feel crowded in an open shopping mall or they may feel perfectly comfortable in a packed concert hall. The experience of crowding in educational settings appears to be related to personal space violation (Epstein and Karlin, 1975). Hall's (1959) typology distinguishes personal distance (eighteen to thirty inches) from social distance (four to twelve feet). Hall suggested that interactions between friends and acquaintances typically occur in the far phase of personal distance, from thirty inches to four feet. Interactions between unacquainted individuals or those conducting informal business transactions tend to occur in the near phase of social distance, from four to seven feet. Hall argued that violations of these social norms lead to emotional discomfort and behaviors designed to restore the appropriate interpersonal distance. Research suggests that numerous variables moderate these distance norms. For example, individuals involved in cooperative group tasks tend to perform better at small (two feet) versus large (five feet) interpersonal distances (Seta, Paulus, and Schkade, 1976). Thus students working on collaborative learning exercises may have a lower threshold for crowding than students listening to a traditional lecture. For classroom designers, this means that social distance does not need to be maintained in collaborative classrooms. Instead, groups can be expected to work together at personal distances of two to four feet without feeling crowded.

Another common objection to collaborative learning activities is that they are too noisy. The impact of noise on learning depends on a range of factors, including the properties of the noise itself (such as loudness and pitch), individual differences, and task characteristics. Although one might guess that noise in the classroom would always inhibit learning, evidence suggests otherwise. In some situations and within normal parameters, noise has either no impact on performance or enhances it. As for the actual noise level in collaborative classrooms, one study of preschool students obtained sound levels above ninety-five decibels in open plan classrooms, prolonged exposure to which can cause permanent auditory damage (Neill and Denham, 1982). In a college environment, however, there is no reason to believe that the volume of group conversation during collaborative activities cannot be held to normal levels (fifty to sixty decibels). Thus it is suggested that designers need not expend any additional resources to reduce noise in collaborative classrooms.

New Frontiers

In addition to pushing traditional lectures out of college classrooms, information technology is pushing the limits of online human communication and collaboration, opening new frontiers for collaborative learning. It is currently possible to conduct a virtual class meeting on the Web, wherein students not only see the slides and other materials as the instructor moves through them but can actually take control of the presentation, directing attention to a specific slide or making a change to a specific document as everyone watches from their remote locations. Sophisticated group support systems allow virtual teams to facilitate brainstorming, polling, negotiation, consensus building, and other group tasks at a distance (Nunamaker, Briggs, and Mittleman, 1999). The pace of adoption can be expected to quicken as universities invest in collaboration technology and as instructors gain more expertise in facilitating online collaboration.

A second frontier opened by the advance of information technology involves the human-centered design of online collaborative workspaces. Putting this in context, what would a virtual collaborative classroom look like? The area of psychology most concerned with interface design is human factors psychology (Sanders and McCormick, 1993). Although the educational and psychological literature includes extensive anecdotal discussions of virtual learning communities (Harasim, Hiltz, Teles, and Turoff, 1997), a scientific understanding of the human-centered design and usability of these applications is only beginning to emerge.

A third major frontier involves the integration of virtual and face-to-face collaborative environments. This thrust can be separated into two major initiatives: facilitating the flow of information between face-to-face and virtual workspaces and supporting the involvement of geographically distributed participants in fixed-site class meetings. Instructors will need to upload information developed during class to online, collaborative applications. Off-campus content experts and remote students will also need to be integrated into the face-to-face sessions using collaboration technology. The classrooms of the future must provide for this seamless flow of information between physical and virtual environments.

Two Examples of Collaborative Learning Spaces

In a chapter on collaborative learning places, it seems appropriate to include some real, working examples. The Studio in the Ryan C. Harris Learning Teaching Center at the University of Dayton is a good example of collaborative classroom design. Digital photographs of the Studio can be viewed through http://spacesforlearning.udayton.edu. Measuring thirty by thirty feet, the Studio was designed to accommodate up to twenty-four students. Although the room is windowless, relatively high ceilings and a double French door designed to make learning activities visible to passers-by reduce perceived crowding. The Studio's traditional fluorescent lamps can be adjusted to shine upward, for indirect, relatively comfortable lighting. The instructor can also control room temperature, and the room is set off from the main thoroughfare, so external noise is generally not a problem. Although well equipped, the Studio makes unobtrusive use of technology. A mobile, interactive white board and some wireless laptops are stored in an adjoining closet and can be accessed quickly when needed. Coat hooks and shelves along one wall allow students to store belongings that may get in the way during collaborative activities. Movable tables allow instructors to configure the room for numerous group tasks. Movable white boards on a ceiling track system not only provide groups with plenty of writing surfaces but can also be arranged to separate the groups physically, providing some level of privacy and reducing distraction. Each semester, faculty members at the University of Dayton are invited to submit a proposal to teach in the Studio, in which they describe how they are going to use the space. Those accepted become part of a users' group and meet regularly to discuss their courses and ways that the Studio can be used to facilitate learning. The development of such user communities centered on specific learning spaces may be an effective means of increasing instructors' place attachment to classrooms.

The University of Dayton is also using an online collaborative application called Lotus QuickPlace to support distributed group work. More information about QuickPlace can be obtained at http://spacesforlearning .udayton.edu. QuickPlaces can be created quickly and accessed by team members immediately via their Web browsers without installing any special software. Each QuickPlace has at least one manager, typically the course instructor, who can modify, customize, and shape the QuickPlace to meet the needs of the team or group. Once they have signed in to their

QuickPlace, students can begin using it to create and edit documents, share files, communicate with their team members, and engage in other collaborative activities.

Final Remarks

When both expository lectures and collaborative learning can take place online, will there even be a need for fixed-site classrooms? This, of course, is a critical question of the Information Age. Will online shopping make grocery stores obsolete? Will e-learning make college classrooms obsolete? Perhaps the best glimpse into the future comes from the business world, where approaches that blend online with face-to-face instruction are quickly replacing earlier distance learning models as businesses rediscover the importance of face-to-face interaction (Rosenberg, 2001). Far from isolating learners and instructors, information technology appears to be bringing them closer together both physically and virtually (Cairncross, 1997). There is good reason to believe that face-to-face interaction will be an even more important component of the learning process in the near future. Downsizing seems very unlikely in a learning environment based on experience, action, service, and collaboration versus information delivery.

Successful universities will provide students and instructors with environments that facilitate collaborative learning. They will stop building large lecture halls and plan instead for small groups of students gathered around tables and engaged in discussion. They will anticipate movement, not just of students and instructors, but of tables, chairs, white boards, data projection, and laptops. They will visualize technology as mobile, unobtrusive, and supportive of collaboration versus information delivery.

Information technology is allowing instructors to finally remove the yoke of expository lecture, freeing them to work with students in more intellectually challenging ways. University administrators must smooth the way for faculty development by providing not only informational and motivational support but also a classroom environment that facilitates collaborative learning. Together, administrators, instructors, and students will define the classrooms of the future.

References

Adams, D., and Hamm, M. *Cooperative Learning: Critical Thinking and Collaboration Across the Curriculum.* (2nd ed.) Springfield, Ill.: Thomas, 1996.

Anderson, C. A., Deuser, W. E., and DeNeve, K. M. "Hot Temperatures, Hostile Affect, Hostile Cognition, and Arousal: Tests of a General Model of Affective Aggression." *Journal of Personality and Social Psychology*, 1995, 21, 434–448.

Bligh, D. A. *What's the Use of Lectures?* San Francisco: Jossey-Bass, 2000.

Brookfield, S. D., and Preskill, S. *Discussion as a Way of Teaching: Tools and Techniques for Democratic Classrooms.* San Francisco: Jossey-Bass, 1999.

Brufee, K. A. *Collaborative Learning: Higher Education, Interdependence, and the Authority of Knowledge.* (2nd ed.) Baltimore: Johns Hopkins University Press, 1999.

Cairncross, F. *The Death of Distance: How the Communications Revolution Will Change Our Lives.* Boston: Harvard Business School Press, 1997.

Coleman, R., Frankel, F., Ritvo, E., and Freeman, B. "The Effect of Fluorescent and Incandescent Illumination upon Repetitive Behavior in Autistic Children." *Journal of Autism and Childhood Schizophrenia,* 1976, 6, 157–162.

Epstein, Y. M., and Karlin, R. A. "Effects of Acute Experimental Crowding." *Journal of Applied Social Psychology,* 1975, 5, 34–53.

Gibson, J. J. *The Senses Considered as Perceptual Systems.* Boston: Houghton Mifflin, 1966.

Gibson, J. J. *The Ecological Approach to Visual Perception.* Boston: Houghton Mifflin, 1979.

Gifford, R. *Environmental Psychology: Principles and Practice.* (2nd ed.) Boston: Allyn & Bacon, 1997.

Glass, G. V., and Smith, M. L. Meta-analysis of Research on the Relationship of Class Size and Achievement. San Francisco: Far West Laboratory for Educational Research and Development, 1978.

Grauerholtz, E., McKenzie, B., and Romero, M. "Beyond These Walls: Teaching Within and Outside the Expanded Classroom Boundaries in the Twenty-First Century." In D. Coleman and R. Khanna (eds.), *Groupware: Technology and Applications.* Upper Saddle River, N.J.: Prentice Hall, 1999.

Hall, E. T. *The Silent Language.* Garden City, N.Y.: Doubleday, 1959.

Harasim, L., Hiltz, S. R., Teles, L., and Turoff, M. *Learning Networks: A Field Guide to Teaching and Learning Online.* Cambridge, Mass.: MIT Press, 1997.

Heller, J. F., Groff, B. D., and Solomon, S. A. "Toward an Understanding of Crowding: The Role of Physical Interaction." *Journal of Personality and Social Psychology,* 1977, 35, 183–190.

Kaplan, S., and Kaplan, R. *Cognition and Environment: Functioning in an Uncertain World.* New York: Praeger, 1982.

Kuller, R., and Lindsten, C. "Health and Behavior of Children in Classrooms With and Without Windows." *Journal of Environmental Psychology,* 1992, 12, 305–317.

Myers, D. G. *Social Psychology.* (6th ed.) New York: McGraw-Hill College, 1999.

Neill, S. R., and Denham, E.J.M. "The Effects of Pre-school Design." *Educational Research,* 1982, 24, 107–111.

Nunamaker, J., Jr., Briggs, R. O., and Mittleman, D. D. "Electronic Meeting Systems: Ten Years of Lessons Learned." In B. A. Pescosolido and R. Aminzade (eds.), *The Social Worlds of Higher Education: Handbook for Teaching in a New Century.* Thousand Oaks, Calif.: Pine Forge Press, 1999.

Prentice-Dunn, S., and Rogers, R. W. "Deindividuation and the Self-Regulation of Behavior." *Journal of Personality and Social Psychology,* 1980, 39, 104–113.

Rosenberg, M. J. *E-Learning: Strategies for Delivering Knowledge in the Digital Age.* New York: McGraw-Hill, 2001.

Sanders, M. S., and McCormick, E. J. *Human Factors Engineering and Design.* (7th ed.) New York: McGraw-Hill, 1993.

Seta, J. J., Paulus, P. B., and Schkade, J. K. "Effects of Group Size and Proximity Under Cooperative and Competitive Conditions." *Journal of Personality and Social Psychology,* 1976, 34, 47–53.

Steele, S. F., and Marshall, S. "On Raising Hopes of Raising Teaching: A Glimpse of Introduction to Sociology in 2005." *Teaching Sociology,* 1996, 24, 1–7.

Tuan, Y. F. *Topophilia.* Upper Saddle River, N.J.: Prentice Hall, 1974.

Weinstein, C. S. "The Physical Environment of School: A Review of the Research." *Review of Educational Research*, 1979, 49, 577–610.

Weinstein, C. S. "Classroom Design as an External Condition for Learning." *Educational Technology*, 1981, 21, 12–19.

Wyon, D. P. "Studies of Children Under Imposed Noise and Heat Stress." *Ergonomics*, 1970, 13, 598–612.

KEN A. GRAETZ *is an associate professor of psychology and director of e-learning at Winona State University.*

MICHAEL J. GOLIBER *is a graduate assistant in psychology and in the Collaboratory in the Ryan C. Harris Learning Teaching Center at the University of Dayton.*

3

*The creation of new learning environments should
embrace both virtual and real spaces. This chapter
explores options for integrating these two modes of
learning and offers e-learning and learning environment
integration and design implications.*

Embracing the Hybrid Model: Working at the Intersections of Virtual and Physical Learning Spaces

Thomas D. Skill, Brian A. Young

Intense public excitement about e-learning and distance education has many institutions of higher education scrambling to stake their claims and establish their reputations in the largely unexplored territory of online learning. Whether it is for profit, public service, or professional prestige, the world of e-learning is dramatically reshaping public perceptions of education. Consequently, many observers have begun to ask some difficult questions about the quality, effectiveness, and cost of these online learning initiatives. In fact, the *Wall Street Journal* provided an in-depth discussion of the issues surrounding the growth and impact of e-learning in a thirty-six-page special report in the March 12, 2001, edition of the paper. One of the primary questions posed to e-learning practitioners focuses on the appropriateness of virtual learning environments: "Can teachers really teach and learners really learn if they are separated by distance or mediated by technologies?" This is a very important question for educators and researchers to address because it pushes at the core of what many believe to be a critical success factor for all learners: the environment for learning.

Although many educators have become increasingly (perhaps even aggressively) vocal over the environmental learning conditions of the virtual world (Cleary, 2001), most have remained almost complacent about the conditions of the physical learning environments where they ply their craft on a near-daily basis and where the vast majority of learners gather (Ehrenkrantz, 2000). Within this context is the goal of this chapter: to provide a series of perspectives on the ways in which we might think about the redesign of physical learning environments and to consider the challenges of integrating the tools and techniques of e-learning into these new learning spaces.

Bruce Jilk, an educational planner and architect, observed that one of the great challenges that we face in reshaping educational environments is rooted in the ways that decision makers envision their role (Fielding, 2001). If we see ourselves as being in the "teaching business," we will tend to make decisions that support the self-serving interests of teachers. If we are in the "learning business," we are more likely to respond to the needs and interests of both students and teachers. As one considers this perspective, Jilk suggests that we should address a fundamental question about the environment for learners: "What, in the past, was an environmental barrier to learning and what enabled learning?" We immediately recognize that this is not an easy question to answer. There are numerous variables to consider, including individual learning styles, pedagogical strategies, and learning objectives, to name just a few. Careful observation and analysis of environmental factors that encourage or inhibit learning are essential tools for identifying meaningful patterns that will inform our designs for future learning spaces.

Although many agree that the traditional classroom is no longer a viable space for learner-centered activities, Jilk (Fielding, 2001) and Roger Schank (Fielding, 1999) take this one step further by envisioning new models made up of community learning spaces that provide a common place where learners will gather for conversation. In fact, Schank, while director of the Institute for Learning Sciences at Northwestern University, publicly expressed his belief that learners should "spend one-third of their day at the computer, one-third talking with others, and one-third making something." Schank's hybrid approach to learning clearly favors a combination of interactive and learning-by-doing strategies.

While many critics' reactions to technology and e-learning may be driven by either discomfort with change or philosophical opposition to distributed ("distance") learning models, past patterns suggest that the likely future will be neither solely online learning nor solely instructor-led classroom learning. (For an in-depth discussion of the philosophical opposition to technology, see Talbott, 1995.) For many of us who have been working with various learning models, it appears that hybrid or blended models most frequently emerge as the most effective learning strategy. This likelihood suggests that the creation of new learning environments should embrace both virtual and real spaces. Understanding how best to integrate these two modes of learning is and will continue to be a significant challenge for educators.

As various hybrid approaches begin to surface in courses and curricula, we fully anticipate that both physical and virtual environmental factors will become key variables in determining the success or failure of these implementation strategies. The challenge is to design learning spaces that do not simply accommodate the need for diverse learning approaches but embrace, empower, and sustain learners of differing capabilities and interests.

When we speak of "integrated learning environments," we are referring to a blended learning experience that combines in-class teaching and learning modalities with robust electronically mediated experiences. This integrated or hybrid approach moves well beyond the concept of bolting a Web site onto a traditional classroom-based course:

1. The integrated hybrid course is carefully redesigned so as to best leverage powerful in-class, face-to-face teaching and learning opportunities with the content richness and interactivity of electronic learning experiences.
2. The e-learning component of the integrated hybrid class emphasizes facilitated "time on task" activities such as virtual teamwork, synchronous communication, and threaded discussions.
3. The redesigned integrated hybrid course moves away from traditional notions of "seat time" by carefully integrating "online" time investment into the "clock hour" contact calculations. Learning outcomes and "time on task" are the new metrics for assessing the integrated hybrid course.
4. The integrated hybrid course emphasizes learner empowerment and responsibility as a key value in the course design. Students are encouraged to take control of their learning through both team-based and independent learning activities. Opportunities for the creation of meaningful, student-controlled learning communities (both in person and virtual) are an essential component in most hybrid courses.

While there are many ways to design integrated virtual and physical learning environments, it is our belief that deriving those designs from sound principles that are viewed by many as enablers of learning will offer the greatest opportunity for long-term sustainability and success. Chickering and Gamson's (1987) "Seven Principles for Good Practice in Undergraduate Education" provides an excellent set of guiding concepts that can inform thinking on the design, construction, and integration of virtual and physical learning environments. These principles were originally intended to help faculty rethink their approaches to teaching; however, they are equally powerful in helping us rethink the design and use of learning environments. Chickering and Ehrmann (1996) applied these principles to the e-learning environment in their article "Implementing the Seven Principles: Technology as Lever." We will explicate their analysis as we explore the integration of real and virtual learning environments.

The following sections outline the seven principles of good practice.

Good Practice Encourages Student-Faculty Contact

A recurring theme in the literature on learning environment design emphasizes the importance of creating spaces that will support relationship building among learners and teachers (Taylor, 2000). Establishing a safe and trusting relationship between students and teachers can be greatly facilitated if the learning environment encourages learners and teachers to interact before, during, and after formal class meetings. Design considerations include conversation-friendly alcoves connected or adjacent to the more formal teaching and learning spaces. If major renovations are planned, consideration should be given to building student-controlled spaces where individual and group work can be conducted and faculty can comfortably engage in conversations with students. The goal might be to design spaces that will allow work begun during class meetings to easily move to adjacent team and independent work areas. These spaces must also allow easy access to information resources through wired or wireless data connections. The ability for students to use the campus communications infrastructure to exchange e-mail, contribute to discussion forums, or visit a teacher during virtual office hours are all key factors in establishing good practices that encourage faculty-student contact.

Good Practice Encourages Cooperation Among Students

The relationship between learning environments and student collaboration is perhaps the most important design element of all. Empowering students to work cooperatively as members of a team is a wonderful aspiration that is very difficult to facilitate if the environment does not support real and virtual collaboration. Students are very busy people who face the same challenges as faculty in trying to find common times and welcoming spaces for working together. Convincing evidence, both empirical and anecdotal, demonstrates the potential for student learning as members of a team (Levine, 1999). (For example, the University of Dayton conducts an annual survey of student uses of information technologies. The results indicate that over 90 percent of respondents use e-mail and other tools on a near daily basis to interact with fellow students on class-related topics.) Designers and educators have been moving rapidly over the last few years to create spaces that support various types of teamwork. While they go by many names—team rooms, study tables, and cybercafés—they all serve the purpose of empowering learners to work collectively in student-controlled spaces. The challenge, however, is in providing a context for learners to become productive and efficient teammates. So, as we attempt to respond with expanded teaming environments, we also need to provide communication tools and resources that will allow students to take full advantage of these spaces. The use of shared calendars for coordinating meeting times and reserving meeting spaces adds much to the learners' experiences, while making the process of coming together more efficient. The development of virtual teaming spaces that allow students to electronically manage their team work, to develop and distribute copies of their individual contributions, and to collaboratively write and edit common documents are enhancements that integrated learning environments must support.

Good Practice Encourages Active Learning

We have explored some of the ways that student-controlled spaces encourage cooperation and active learning. The critical connection between physical spaces and active learning cannot be overstated. Teachers, curriculum designers, and learners scale their aspirations for learning experiences based on the constraints imposed by the learning environment. If the learning situation lacks sufficient space for group-driven activities, that learning option is not considered. If learning might be enhanced through the use of multimedia materials, we will integrate those items only if they are readily accessible. Field trips to campus computer labs are not active learning activities—they are inhibitors because many faculty view the cost of getting access as exceeding the benefit. Active learning can best be encouraged when the space and resources are routinely available for learners in the places where they gather.

Because there are very real constraints on physical learning spaces at almost every institution, the opportunity does exist to accelerate the use of virtual learning environments as a way of rapidly responding to the need for new spaces that allow for active learning. Integrating electronic simulations, games, and project-based tasks with in-person activities serves to engage students on many levels. The use of electronic discussions as the basis for in-person group conversations serves a dual purpose of encouraging interactive, time-on-task actions while elevating the level of public discussion on a topic. However, instructor-guided activities are only a small part of active learning. Assignments that blend collaboration with task-intensive activities are among the most fruitful learning approaches. It is not unusual for "general education" history classes to assign student teams to work on the research, design, and construction of Web sites on an assigned history topic. This approach fits very closely with Roger Schank's recommendation that students divide their day in thirds among computer work, conversation, and construction. The added benefit is that the collaboratively produced Web site becomes a public or semipublic form of scholarship. As we think of ways to integrate active learning into the real and virtual curriculum, it may be beneficial to expand this approach to include learning spaces that support collaboration and public displays of student accomplishments. When students engage in public scholarship, they are much more likely to spend time revising and editing their work (Bass, n.d.).

Good Practice Gives Prompt Feedback

Feedback seems to be almost too harsh a term when paired with the concepts of learning environments and learning communities. Many communication scholars contend that feedback and communication are one and the same (Cusella, 1980). For learners to achieve at high levels, they must engage in frequent communications with their mentors. While the traditional classroom models of recitation, critique, and final grade may fit the strict definition of feedback, most educators today recognize that constructive conversations are a much more potent model for learning. Frequent conversations in settings that are conducive to learning are even better. We are discovering that learning environments that move away from the traditional "sage on the stage" lecture model may be a good place to start those conversations. The great challenge for many educators (whose primary role is to engage learners) and designers (whose primary role is to develop the spaces where learners gather) is to find a way to create larger, more flexible learning spaces so that multiple activities can happen at the same time. Learning environments that can quickly shift from a large group presentation to a series of small work teams will encourage faculty to rethink their pedagogy. And if those spaces permit guided independent learning and the opportunity for directed one-on-one feedback, the empowered learner may move to the next level of achievement and success.

As students move from formal to informal learning spaces (academic buildings to residential spaces), it is extremely important that communication and feedback are readily available. For this reason, the technological infrastructure of a campus needs to provide the tools and access from nearly everywhere to everywhere. The concept of anytime, anywhere learning drives this perspective.

Good Practice Emphasizes Time on Task

Whether it is reading and reflecting, discussing and debating, writing and analyzing, or creating and building, time on task is the critical key to learner success. Each of these activities requires spaces that support and encourage the investment of time. Since time on task involves activities that include all forms of learning, the design of physical spaces to support time on task requires a systems view of the learning environment. The outmoded Industrial Age model of education as a series of seat time requirements stands as a significant barrier to learning—but not an insurmountable one. Some observers of today's college-age learners contend that they are most eager to learn when they are deeply immersed in a learning environment (Tapscott, 1998). Formal teaching spaces such as traditional classrooms may not provide the motivating environment for learning or time-on-task activities, so the effectiveness of the class is apt to suffer if these spaces are the only setting available to educators. However, virtual environments that engage students in interactive simulations or real environments that blend learning with socializing are frequently very effective at putting learners on task for extended periods of time. Should we invest in multimedia environments like the Virtual CAVE (which provides a realistic computer-simulated experience such as flying an aircraft) on our campuses? Probably not, but we may want to consider increasing the amount of space on campus available to students for the creation of time-on-task learning activities. This may

mean larger living spaces so that students can create their versions of learning studios. Other approaches may involve creating virtual labs that mimic
real environments, developing learning environments with corporate partners in off-site facilities, or enabling client consultations for service learning projects with remote teleconferencing capabilities. It also might involve
a new definition of living and learning spaces, which could lead us to think
differently about public, semipublic, and private spaces in the traditional
academic or student activities buildings.

Good Practice Communicates High Expectations

Excellent work is enabled by workplaces where excellence can be achieved.
While critics of the traditional educational model might define it as "learning as torture" (Tapscott, 1998, p. 147) because of its highly structured,
teacher-centered orientation, an argument could be made that the more tor-
turous aspect of the model may be rooted in the inflexible physical environment that also characterizes this approach. Some students can achieve
excellence in just such an environment, but for many others this approach
will not encourage them to succeed.

Setting high expectations does not mean that all students must achieve
at the same level or follow the same path for learning. The more flexible the
environment for learning and the more numerous the paths available for
students to pursue excellence, the greater the likelihood of student achievement. This approach requires a blending of multiple methods in e-learning
integrated with a learning-objectives-driven curriculum. As instructors
increase the flexibility of the course requirements and pedagogical methods, the demand for larger and more flexible learning environments will
increase.

Good Practice Respects Diverse Talents and Ways of Learning

A great many strategies and tactics are available for responding to the needs
of a diverse group of learners. Perhaps our greater challenge is in trying to
find ways to efficiently and productively implement and sustain these
approaches. At many institutions, it frequently seems as though faculty
alone are tasked with identifying and implementing solutions that will
accommodate the diverse learning needs of their students. And though
more and more institutions are trying to help instructors address these challenges through the use of learning assistance professionals, we rarely seem
to identify the design or conditions of learning environments as equally critical factors for learner achievement.

The implementation of good practices that truly respect and support
diverse talents and ways of learning requires a collaborative strategy that
involves curricular changes, learning environment modifications, and

technological support. Although many institutions have adopted a combination of curriculum and technology innovations, the limitations created by inadequate or inflexible facilities significantly reduce the likelihood of success. The empowerment of teachers in creating and supporting spaces for learning is a critical success factor. Many institutions have relegated the design, renovation, and maintenance of learning spaces to facilities people, but we have found that many of the individuals in these operations are very eager to work with faculty as equal members of the design team in an effort to arrive at solutions that are both cost-effective and highly engaging to our learners.

Moving Forward and Implementing Change

Limited resources for renovations and technology, the incredible demands of time and energy required to plan and implement space changes and technological solutions, and the lack of available space to do the job right are nearly constant restrictions at most institutions. Yet it seems that our campuses are in a perpetual state of reconstruction. At a workshop at the University of Dayton in November 2000, Parker Palmer suggested that one can quickly judge how greatly an institution values its teaching mission by simply visiting a typical campus classroom and observing its condition. We nurture and gently care for things that we value.

As we move forward in defining and implementing the convergence of virtual and physical learning environments, Parkash Nair (2000) has identified fifteen trends that have potential implications for facility designers. We will cover just a few of these items in this chapter, but the full report can be accessed through http://spacesforlearning.udayton.edu. Nine of these trends are very relevant to higher education:

- *Ubiquitous computing:* Access to electronically accessible resources that support learning is no longer a "learning bonus." The computer is an essential tool that must be available on demand and wherever we expect to support learners.
- *Wireless networking and robust Internet access:* It is all about access. Wireless allows for untethered use of information while also reducing infrastructure costs. High-speed Internet access will continue to grow in importance as more items—from text to multimedia materials—become available online. The cost of bandwidth will drop, but the need to continually expand capacity will put pressure on limited budgets.
- *Technology-intensive teaching and learning:* Residential campuses across North America and Europe are not going to shut their doors and become "online U." However, they will continue to develop and deploy a wide variety of e-learning materials. Blended models—with some in-class and some online work—will be commonplace in many courses.

- *Emphasis on informal learning:* Learning is happening away from the class-room and this trend will grow. The demand for more informal spaces for learners will grow along with it.
- *Deemphasis on the classroom:* The classroom is no longer the center of the learning universe. Traditional "teaching boxes" must be redesigned to support collaborative and self-directed learning.
- *Imaginative furniture design:* Work surfaces and related furniture that support active learning and computing will become essential to the success of the new learning environment.
- *Emphasis on service learning:* The integration of service with learning and leadership development is growing rapidly at many institutions. Whether moving from campus to community or bringing the community to cam-pus, space usage will continue to be a key issue.
- *Student-created products for business:* Student business ventures will become an important active learning tactic. Resources to sustain these ini-tiatives will involve the need for new kinds of learning spaces and new technological applications.
- *New learning partnerships:* Engaging with corporate, government, or insti-tutional partners on shared learning journeys will require new approaches to curriculum design and learning environments.

These trends indicate that much will continue to change as educators attempt to address the complex requirements for learning-centered envi-ronments. And while much is known about learner needs for space and resources, it is very difficult to accurately predict what will be needed for specific groups of learners at any given time. With this thought in mind, the consensus among many architects, planners, and educators is this: *design for flexibility.* This recommendation has a number of basic strategies:

- Larger spaces are more flexible than smaller spaces.
- Movable and demountable partitions allow for space reconfigurations within the context of the learning requirements.
- With enough spaces, teachers and students can control the flexibility of the environment to meet the learning needs of the moment.
- Building design can allow for spaces to become a "laboratory for their own evolution" (Ehrenkrantz, 2000).

In the final analysis, the extent to which we can succeed as educators and learners in a learning environment that pushes us to work at the inter-sections of virtual and physical spaces will be determined by our capacity to abandon the old teacher-student behavior scripts where students sit and teachers talk. Some of our biggest challenges will be in rewriting that script for learners and teachers alike.

The hybrid model is an opportunity for educators and students to col-laboratively participate in the creation of new "learning scripts" where engagement and empowerment are key components in both virtual and physical learning environments. With emphasis on learner outcomes, this combination extends learning beyond the classroom in ways that greatly enrich and enliven the experience for students at all levels and abilities.

References

Bass, R. "Engines of Inquiry: Teaching, Technology, and Learner-Centered Approaches to Culture and History." [http://spacesforlearning.udayton.edu].

Chickering, A., and Ehrmann, S. C. "Implementing the Seven Principles: Technology as Lever." *AAHE Bulletin,* Oct. 1996, pp. 3–6.

Chickering, A., and Gamson, Z. "Seven Principles for Good Practice in Undergraduate Education." *AAHE Bulletin,* March 1987, pp. 3–7.

Cleary, S. "The Downside: Why Some Critics Give Web-Based Education Less-Than-Stellar Grades." *Wall Street Journal,* Mar. 12, 2001, p. R32.

Cusella, L. P. "The Effects of Feedback on Intrinsic Motivation: A Propositional Extension of Cognitive Evaluation Theory from an Organizational Communication Perspective." In D. Nimmo (ed.), *Communication Yearbook 4.* New Brunswick, N.J.: Transaction Book, 1980.

Ehrenkrantz, E. "Planning for Flexibility, Not Obsolescence." Ehrenkrantz Eckstut & Kuhn Architects, 2000. [http://spacesforlearning.udayton.edu].

Fielding, R. "The Death of the Classroom, Learning Cycles and Roger Schank," 1999. [http://spacesforlearning.udayton.edu].

Fielding, R. "Amsterdam Watershed: An Interactive Forum on Innovative Alternatives in Learning Environments," 2001. [http://spacesforlearning.udayton.edu].

Levine, J. (ed.). *Learning Communities: New Structures, New Partnerships for Learning.* Center for the Study of the Freshman Year Experience series, no. 26. Columbia: University of South Carolina, 1999.

Nair, P. "Schools for the Twenty-First Century," 2000. [http://spacesforlearning.udayton.edu].

Talbott, S. L. *The Future Does Not Compute.* Sebastopol, Calif.: O'Reilly, 1995.

Tapscott, D. *Growing Up Digital.* New York: McGraw-Hill, 1998.

Taylor, A. "Programming and Design of Schools Within the Context of Community," 2000. [http://spacesforlearning.udayton.edu].

THOMAS D. SKILL is associate provost for academic technology, co-director of the Learning Village, and professor of communication at the University of Dayton.

BRIAN A. YOUNG is vice president and CIO, Division of Information Technology and Academic Learning Environments, Hobart and William Smith Colleges.

4

The knowledge economy is ushering in new attitudes about teaching and learning. As a result, different kinds of furniture are being specified for the classroom. These are more flexible and comfortable and do more to accommodate technology and information. Furniture also now plays a role in making learning environments more fun and dynamic, even more inspirational.

The Impact of Changes in Teaching and Learning on Furniture and the Learning Environment

Paul Cornell

Furniture is both tool and environment. As with every artifact, it is designed and built with a purpose in mind. It is no different for learning environments. Until recently these were built to enable a teacher to deliver a message to a large group, which sat in silence, dutifully listening and taking notes. Rooms were rectangular or wedge-shaped, and the focus—and attention—was directed to the front where the instructor exercised complete control of the pace, content, and sequence of activities. Teaching varied little, so the furniture was optimized and bolted in place.

This educational system suited the industrial economy. It matched the economic, social, technological, and demographic needs of the times. A literate and competent workforce was provided for hierarchical and centrally controlled organizations. This workforce contributed to an unprecedented period of growth and prosperity in the industrialized countries. Despite the research of Maria Montessori and John Dewey about better ways to teach, "stand and deliver" remained the dominant design for all educational environments—from young child to seasoned executive.

Today, the industrial economy is history. In his groundbreaking books *Future Shock* (1970) and *The Third Wave* (1980), Alvin Toffler was one of the first to popularize the notion that our economy—and hence our lives, work, and behavior—was undergoing tremendous change. The industrial economy has given way to the knowledge economy. Economic power no longer resides in land, natural resources, or capital but in knowledge, networks, and relationships. Over 59 percent of the workforce consists of knowledge workers, that is, knowledge and information are the raw material *and* product of their efforts (Stewart, 1997). But *all* work has a strong knowledge component. Witness autonomous teams of factory workers deciding about product improvements.

Successful leaders realize they need learning organizations. Successful educators realize they need to prepare a different breed of citizen. In a sense, work needs to become more like school, where learning is an expected part of the job. And conversely, school needs to become more like work, anticipating the kinds of skills and knowledge students will require for a happy and successful life. Work activity, or pedagogy in the case of education, has changed drastically. New methods require new tools and environments. Since furniture is a tool with a specific function, it too must change.

Pedagogical Shift

Much has been written about how teaching methods are changing. The change is driven in large part by economic need. However, other contributing factors include improved understanding of cognition (Gardner, 1983; Reber, 1993), attitudes regarding the nature of knowledge (Davenport and Prusak, 1998; Gardner, 1999), the role of context in learning and behavior (Brown and Duguid, 1997; Suchman, 1987), and the importance of social learning (Ormrod, 1998; Wenger, 1999)—just to name a few. This research and its impact is too vast to review in depth here, but has been summarized in Table 4.1. This table addresses the shift taking place in education today.

The tenets of the emerging model are not new, but our circumstances have changed. The industrial era begot an educational environment that has been in place since the late 1800s. That era passed years ago, but we struggle to shake free of its legacy. It is time to move on.

Table 4.1.   Emerging Paradigm of Teaching and Learning

From an Industrial Economy	*To a Knowledge Economy*
Passive learners	Active learners
Directed learning	Facilitated learning
Knowledge revealed	Knowledge discovered
Explicit knowledge	Explicit and tacit
Knowledge is discrete	Knowledge is embedded
Single assessments	Multiple assessments
Single intelligence	Multiple intelligences
Instructor technology	Ubiquitous technology
Alone	Alone and together
Just in case	Just in time
Content	Content and process
Linear and planned	Planned and chaotic

User-Centered Design

Any designer worth hiring takes into account the needs and wishes of the intended audience. The human factors profession made a science of this in the 1940s, and in Europe the ergonomics community goes back even further in history. More recently, *user-centered* design has gained popularity. The essence of the idea is that the needs of the end user should constantly drive design. When it comes to furniture, we need to be concerned with two kinds of users—instructors and learners. Instructors include teachers, professors, and trainers, and learners include children, teens, adults, or employees.

Most furniture design focuses on functional need, such as flexibility, mobility, and wire management. It focuses on helping the user achieve a goal, be it relaxation, entertainment, education, or work. In a user-centered approach, functionality is just one of at least four dimensions to consider. Another design objective is comfort, safety, and health. The design should maintain if not promote well-being and quality of life. No design should be harmful. A third dimension is usability. The intended purpose and operation should be obvious to all users, hopefully with little or no training. The intention is to prevent accidents and optimize use. And fourth, the design should have psychological appeal. The user should feel motivated to use the design over and over again.

Unlike Maslow's, this is not a hierarchy of needs. The dimensions are not additive but multiplicative—poor performance on one undermines the performance of the overall system. Furniture must address all four simultaneously or the efficacy of the design is in question. As described by Duke (1998), researchers tend to focus on one or two areas. In practice, all must be present.

Implications of User-Centered Design on Furniture

All four dimensions are important to furniture design, but that is not the total story. The best solution is one in which furniture, architecture, and technology are designed to work seamlessly and harmoniously. McVey (1996) provides an excellent overview of how these three come together. In the following, however, the focus will be on furniture.

Comfort, Safety, and Health. The intent of addressing comfort, safety, and health needs is to promote well-being and minimize distractions. The new pedagogy outlined in Table 4.1 has actually improved classroom ergonomics. The "stand and deliver" method required uninterrupted sitting for long periods. This can result in drowsiness and muscle fatigue, especially in unupholstered, nonarticulating chairs. No *static* posture is good. The more engaging process on the right of Table 4.1 typically requires students to be more active physically and mentally, eliminating static postures.

Even when we sit, we should still be able to move. Chairs that have flexible backs are preferred because they allow greater occupant movement and positioning. The tension in the back should be adjustable to accommodate the large and small user. Upholstery with adequate foam—usually in excess of one-inch thickness—will reduce pressure points on the back, buttocks, and legs. A waterfall front seat edge is better than a right angle for circulation and comfort. A seat height adjustment range of sixteen to twenty-one inches is available on many chairs. Other recommendations on chair dimensions can be found in the 1988 American National Standards Institute guideline, which is still the best available on the subject.

Regarding tables, a fixed height of 28.5 inches provides the best surface for multiple uses. It can be used for writing, drawing, computer use, or collaboration. Fixed-height tables are simpler and less expensive than adjustable tables, and always align when nested side by side.

For dedicated computer use, an adjustable-height table should be considered. Three factors contribute to the need for adjustability: task duration, posture activity level, and availability of an adjustable-height chair. The longer the task and the more static the posture, the greater the need for adjustability. An adjustable-height chair will often serve, however. Adjustable keyboard shelves may also be considered.

Tables and chairs get most of the attention because people sit and lean on them. But cupboards, carts, shelves, audiovisual units, and display screens also have to be carefully designed. All mobile elements should be on casters, and lockable casters may be appropriate for tables and carts. Flooring is a consideration because casters for carpet are different from those for hard surfaces. Even with casters, some units may be too heavy or too dangerous to move around. For example, AV cabinets tend to have a high center of gravity that makes them prone to tipping over if care is not taken.

Usability. Clarity, ease of use, access, and control are all part of usability. A product may be tremendously functional and wonderfully ergonomic, but if it is not *usable,* if users do not understand how it works, then it is a failure. They need to understand its operation and feel empowered to use it.

Usability can be achieved in several ways. The best is to follow industry standards or common practice (such as "rightie-tightie, leftie-loosie" or the P R N D L order of gears on an automatic transmission). If no such model exists, the design should be intuitively obvious. This is problematic due to the diversity of cultures and experience in our society. Few things are obvious to everyone. A third course is to provide labels or instructions with the product. Fourth is training. Especially with furniture, a quick demonstration is often all that is needed.

Unfortunately, furniture controls have little standardization. The operation and location of levers, buttons, and knobs vary within as well as between manufacturers. Labels and trial and error often overcome this—provided users are encouraged to try things out. Experience shows that instructors and students take the room as is, rarely moving tables or even adjusting seat height. Making the functions easier, providing training or orientation, and posting suggested room layouts all help people make better use of the environment.

Psychological Appeal. Learning is a social process and is often informal. It is no longer about showing up at a specified time and place, it is about being at the right place at the right time. Networking and relationships are key to learning. Thus, more than ever, the environment must now serve as a magnet, drawing people in. When people feel comfortable and valued they will come, stay, and return. Learning communities will result.

The space predisposes people to certain kinds of behavior. A fixed, "eyes forward" arrangement says the environment is one for listening, not interaction. Putting furniture on casters indicates that the room is reconfigurable. Chairs that are adjustable convey a concern for the users and their comfort. Tables arranged in clusters, facing one another, suggest collaboration. Table size and shape also have an impact. People can sit on all sides and collaborate at a table that is thirty or more inches deep. Not so at an eighteen-inch table. Round and curvilinear tables also promote collaboration.

The fit and finish of furnishings also convey a message. Boardrooms, with their leather chairs and polished mahogany tables, certainly say something about the users. Dull, institutional, and otherwise ugly furnishings do not motivate people to stay. Nicely appointed furnishings convey a message of trust and respect that is reciprocal between owner and visitor.

Functionality. The user-centered design criterion that gets the most attention is functionality. Furniture should help the instructor and student achieve their goals using the methods and tools of their choice. Furniture should facilitate learning, not just be a place to sit. To support the emerging paradigm listed in Table 4.1, the architecture, furniture, and technology must be integrated to provide the following capabilities:

Fold-n-go. Users—instructors and students—need to be able to quickly and easily reconfigure rooms from lecture to small group and back again. The unused equipment needs to be easily put away.

Plug-n-play. Access to technology needs to be provided for students as well as instructors. Power and data connections should be ubiquitous, without hugging the walls for connectivity. "Plugging in" may be physical or wireless.

Say-n-see. Instructors and students need to be able to present, modify, record, and retrieve information within the classroom. Electronic and nonelectronic presentation both need to be massively supported.

Relate-n-reflect. Student collaboration—from dyads up to groups of fifteen or more—needs to be supported. But so does solitary concentration. Somewhere within the environment, both must be available.

Inspire-n-invite. Motivation plays a major part in learning. Environments that are fun, energetic, and enjoyable will yield better learning opportunities.

Fold-n-go. Simply pushing unused furniture to the side does not work, as it is messy and wastes space. It is better if the furniture folds, compresses, or is designed to store. Casters generally work best, but lightweight construction may allow stacking. Square footage per student needs to increase from the twelve to fifteen common in dense-pack classrooms to twenty-two to twenty-five square feet or higher. The floor needs to be flat, with no terraces or platforms.

Plug-n-play. Instructors typically get all the technology, but now students need it too. Until wireless connectivity becomes ubiquitous, table-height access is best for laptops. Ports and duplexes can be mounted in the table or provided in freestanding posts. Floor boxes are less convenient but workable. Laptops are small compared to desktop computers, but they still require more work surface per student than paper and pencil—thirty inches wide by twenty-four deep minimum. Most tablet-arm chairs and student desks are too small for laptops, but can be made to work if books and notes are not required.

Pending advancements in battery and wireless technology, designers will be hard-pressed to simultaneously provide both fold-n-go and plug-n-play. In the meantime, table-based modular data and power are available. With the proper building infrastructure, this allows facilities managers to reconfigure and power up tables in thirty minutes or less.

Say-n-see. Instructors are always provided with the tools to present information. Increasingly, students need this ability too, especially for small-group sessions. During lectures, students take notes, writing on pads on a horizontal surface. With teams, the notes are large and vertical, so everyone can see. Teams share knowledge, create ideas, and solve problems. Their activities need to be recorded, displayed, and retrieved. Mobile display boards and computer projectors allow groups to take notes in the middle of the room rather than along a wall. They also serve as a visual barrier between groups. Students may wish to remove tables and simply gather their chairs around the board.

Relate-n-reflect. Collaboration is the biggest pedagogical factor driving change in classroom design. It is why rooms are becoming larger and more flexible. It is the chief reason for the shift from desks to tables. With tables, students can face one another and documents and materials can be shared. Trapezoidal and other nonrectangular shapes enable different kinds of spatial arrangements for collaboration. Chairs without tablets are more flexible and generally more comfortable.

But some of our best learning, achieving those "ah-ha" experiences, occurs during periods of solitude and quiet. Privacy is usually provided by the architecture, being remote, or by background noise. Mobile easels and lightweight screens or cabinetry can also provide privacy, at least visually.

Inspire-n-invite. In user-centered design, psychological appeal addresses the user's emotional reaction to a product. In learning environments, this not only makes users feel good, it has the functional benefit of improving learning. Environments can create a more relaxed, sociable setting by including lounge seating, sofas, standing-height tables and coffee tables. A Starbucks-like atmosphere is more conducive to networking and informal learning than a typical classroom is.

The user-centered approach suggests that design is multidimensional. While functional requirements are usually the most pressing and challenging, all issues must be incorporated into the design.

An Experimental Case

User-centered design principles were put to use in a study of college accounting classes (Cornell and Martin, 1999). The experiment was driven by the faculty's desire for more in-class collaboration and visual display. Student desks were replaced with 20x60-inch tables and lightweight chairs. Mobile easels provided additional markerboard surface. A cart housed a computer and document camera while another held an overhead projector. Information could be displayed in three ways simultaneously—projector, overhead, and markerboard. Twelve professors taught fourteen different classes. Video ethnography recorded behavior, and surveys and focus groups provided student and faculty feedback. Time-lapse video recorded a full semester, and four surveys were administered.

Students found the furniture to be more comfortable than the desks and were observed to assume a variety of postures. Student and faculty made use of the flexibility, but the frequency varied considerably between faculty members. Two preferred lecture format and had students arrange it for them in advance. Others created large aisles, U-shaped layouts, and small group clusters. They would then work the room, getting out among the students rather than remaining on stage. This improved student interaction and engagement. Instructors were often observed using two or three of the displays, but for different purposes. The computer projector displayed the prepared lecture notes, the overhead often showed the schedule, and the markerboard was used in answering questions. The layout of the space when students arrived had a bearing on their participation. In lecture format, students appeared to get set for listening. In cluster layout, students arrived and started conversations.

This study is significant in several ways. First, all four aspects of user-centered design were assessed. Second, professors varied significantly in how they taught, supporting the need for flexibility. Third, what was taught had a strong bearing on how it was taught. For example, the class on accounting standards is mostly memorization so student collaboration is not helpful. Fourth, different display media lend themselves to different uses. All serve a purpose. And finally, the environment had an unpredictable impact on behavior. Professors had not anticipated their own "working the room" and multidisplay behavior. As a result of this experience, several said they were going to experiment even further in the following semester.

Breaking Patterns

In addition to field research, insight can also be gleaned from the actions of leading institutions and organizations that are creating Knowledge Age learning environments.

Take, for example, the Massachusetts Institute of Technology's Department of Aeronautics and Astronautics. Professors discovered their graduates took a long time to come up to speed once hired. After considerable study, MIT determined it needed to change the curriculum to be more like work and less like college. With a new emphasis on corporate-sponsored, project-based learning, the department realized the classroom building was inadequate. It remodeled, creating more project rooms and informal meeting areas, a large project studio, and new lab space. It also made the space more open, replacing solid walls with glass. This enabled students to participate vicariously in other projects. It also aided in informal communication.

The inspiring story of Bill Strickland and the Manchester Craftsmen's Guild provides an excellent example of how the environment sets the tone for the entire learning experience. Located in Pittsburgh, Manchester's target audience is high school students who have been unsuccessful in school. Despite their often troubled past, these students are treated with respect and dignity, and much is expected in return. Most not only graduate but go on to very successful careers. There is much to be said about the program and its philosophy, but of interest here is the use of the environment. Office furniture is used in place of standard high school desks. This provides a comfort advantage, but more important to Strickland, conveys a professional look that students respond to. Their demeanor and performance is more professional as a result.

Aquinas College's Masters of Management program is directed at professionals seeking an advanced degree. One of the benefits is the way it enables employees from different companies to collaborate and work together on neutral ground. The classroom building that housed the program did not support this behavior, and most students remained on site only during class. A renovation was an opportunity to create team and communal spaces, including a piazza in the center with social and eating areas. In the classrooms, stacking chairs were replaced with more comfortable office chairs. Student tables were replaced with occasional tables, many of which had power and data ports.

Corporate learning centers also leverage space. At one large business-consulting firm's center for professional development, all new employees attend a three-week training regimen. The corporate processes, procedures, and tools are acquired, but just as important, so is the corporate culture. Most spaces are reconfigurable to support lectures, small groups, individual study, simulations, and computer labs. Much of the furniture can fold, nest, or stack for quick reconfiguration and compact storage. To facilitate knowledge transfer, the areas are made to look like workspaces and customer offices. What is the outcome of this attention to detail? When newly trained employees finally report to the office, they already have a worldwide network of Andersen colleagues—their fellow "boot camp" attendees. And all this after just three weeks.

Boeing faced a challenge when it merged with McDonnell-Douglas— the new company had two cultures and two management teams spread throughout North America. It established the Boeing Leadership Center to develop a new class of leaders. A mix of spaces provides a variety of settings conducive to teaching, talking, and socializing. Some areas are formal while others are almost residential. But none look like a typical office. The intent is to provide a setting for the leadership of the company to learn and network—and create a new culture in the process.

The Steelcase University Learning Center is a resource for the company and its dealers. A variety of spaces support formal and informal learning, lecture and collaboration, teamwork and solitary study, quiet and noisy activities, and high- and low-tech interactions. These are provided in sufficient number to allow visitors to select what is best for them. With the exception of technology hubs, all elements are easy for users to move. Technology access is within the length of a patch cord everywhere in the building except the cafeteria. The result is a highly dynamic, energized space that serves as a hub for the organization.

The Role of Furniture in Knowledge Age Learning Environments

The purpose of a learning environment is unchanged, but nothing else remains the same. Society needs citizens who are not just literate but able to continuously learn and grow. Companies need workers skilled at research, interpersonal interactions, technology, and adaptation. Teaching methods now emphasize more collaboration, computer use, and social learning. Learners need to be treated as individuals, with their needs, strengths, and weaknesses accounted for within the curriculum. At the root of all these is our economic march toward the Knowledge Age.

To accommodate these changes the physical environment needs to be bigger, more flexible, provide ubiquitous access to technology, promote interaction and a sense of community, enable formal and informal learning, and convey a sense of energy. The environment should be a place people want to be, not a place they have to be. They should be motivated by fun and enjoyment as much as by a desire to learn.

For its part, furniture needs to be more comfortable, adjustable, intuitive, reconfigurable, technology-capable, compressible, and attractive. When its design incorporates ergonomics, usability, and functionality, furniture will help teachers and students achieve their learning objectives. Making furniture user-centered will enhance the overall experience. In the knowledge economy, where learning is not only continuous but also more informal and serendipitous, anything that makes the experience more positive will also increase learning. If properly designed and placed, furniture is more than a place to sit; it can be a strategic asset.

References

American National Standards Institute. *Human Factors Engineering of Visual Display Terminal Workstations.* (ANSI/HFS 100–1988). Santa Monica, CA: Human Factors Society, 1988.

Brown, J. S., and Duguid, P. *The Social Life of Information.* Boston: Harvard Business School Press, 1997.

Cornell, P., and Martin, S. "Replacing Desks with Tables: The Impact on Classroom Behavior." Paper presented at Learning Environments Symposium, Virginia Tech, Dec. 1999.

Davenport, T., and Prusak, L. *Working Knowledge.* Boston: Harvard Business School Press, 1998.

Duke, D. *Does It Matter Where Our Children Learn?* Charlottesville: Thomas Jefferson Center for Educational Design, University of Virginia, 1998.

Gardner, H. *Frames of Mind.* New York: Basic Books, 1983.

Gardner, H. *The Disciplined Mind.* New York: Simon & Schuster, 1999.

McVey, G. "Ergonomics and the Learning Environment." In D. Jonassen (ed.), *Handbook of Research for Education Communications and Technology.* New York: Macmillan, 1996.

Ormrod, J. E. *Educational Psychology.* Upper Saddle River, N.J.: Prentice Hall, 1998.

Reber, A. *Implicit Learning and Tacit Knowledge.* Oxford, England: Oxford University Press, 1993.

Stewart, T. *Intellectual Capital.* New York: Doubleday, 1997.

Suchman, L. *Plans and Situated Actions.* Cambridge, England: Cambridge University Press, 1987.

Toffler, A. *Future Shock.* New York: Bantam Books, 1970.

Toffler, A. *The Third Wave.* New York: Bantam Books, 1980.

Wenger, E. *Communities of Practice.* Cambridge, England: Cambridge University Press, 1999.

PAUL CORNELL, PH.D., is vice president of product development and marketing at Vecta, a contract furniture manufacturer located in Grand Prairie, Texas.

5

The effective creation of spaces conducive to learning calls for a new level of campus collaboration that will yield exciting and rejuvenating spaces that no one group could conceive in isolation.

Navigating the White Waters of Collaborative Work in Shaping Learning Environments

Deborah J. Bickford

> It would be very interesting to record photographically, not the stages of a painting, but its metamorphosis. One would see perhaps by what course a mind finds its way toward the crystallization of its dream.
>
> —Picasso

> As leaders, we play a crucial role in selecting the melody, setting the tempo, establishing the key, and inviting the players. But that is all we can do. The music comes from something we cannot direct, from a unified whole created among the players—a relational holism that transcends separateness. In the end, when it works, we sit back, amazed and grateful.
>
> —Margaret Wheatley

Pablo Picasso and leadership author Margaret Wheatley both recognize the mystery and challenge involved in crystallizing an idea and making it become a reality. That process is even more miraculous (and challenging) when it represents the confluence and collaboration of many different minds. Such is the situation faced in navigating the white waters of the collaborative work needed in shaping learning environments, the topic of this chapter. The white water metaphor aptly applies because many factors or rocks must be noticed and negotiated in the process of creating productive learning spaces.

New Directions for Teaching and Learning, no. 92, Winter 2002 © Wiley Periodicals, Inc.

In the example of creating a new classroom, the interests and needs of faculty and students engaged in learning must certainly be taken into account, but also at stake are the interests and needs of the staff scheduling the space, the facilities managers who have a role in the creation of the space, the crew responsible for maintaining the space, the budgeting office responsible for managing supporting funds, even the development office for raising the money in the first place. The classroom, in short, has many stakeholders. Just as an unnoticed rock in the rapids poses a danger, failing to acknowledge and work through competing interests in the learning space planning process can dash hopes for the creation of vibrant learning spaces.

This chapter attempts to capture the metamorphosis of learning spaces from concept to reality, while trying to shed light on Wheatley's notion of the music coming "from something we cannot direct, from a unified whole created among the players." The question is, how do we get to that unified whole?

The chapter will focus on two themes. First is a brief description of how the stakeholders in the process, the different groups concerned in the process of creating or renovating learning spaces, often come from different university subcultures, speak different languages, and have conflicting perspectives, needs, and desires for the project, and how failing to create a process to draw their interests and needs into creative tension and resolution will result in the creation of spaces that do not effectively support learning. This state of missed opportunity is all the more troublesome given that campus spaces may be renovated only once every thirty years, if then, and new construction is expected to last even longer. In short, not taking into account the needs and perspectives of key stakeholders to the process is very risky, with serious and lasting consequences.

Second, the chapter offers suggestions on how to create a process by which these competing needs and interests can be harnessed to create learning environments that support learning while being able to be maintained, financed, and sustained. To create true learning spaces requires the development of collaborative structures and processes unprecedented on most campuses. Campuses must move from structures and processes based on enclaves of expertise and specialization of labor (faculty teach, students learn, and facilities managers create and maintain the classroom) to systems that enable organizational learning to take place. Drawing on the rich literature on cross-functional product development teams, the chapter offers practical ideas to shape the process by which useful learning spaces can be created on campuses.

Learning Environment Stakeholders

The concept of stakeholders is a useful framework for identifying key constituents in designing learning spaces. A stakeholder is seen as "any group or individual who can affect or is affected by the achievement of an

Figure 5.1. Learning Spaces Stakeholders

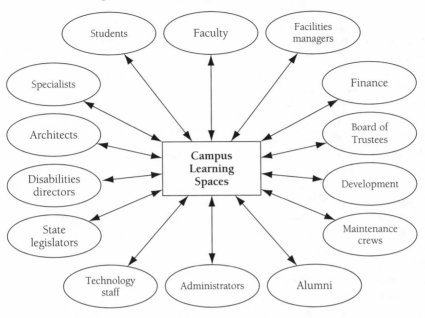

There exist many stakeholders to the development of campus learning spaces, with competing interests.

organization's purpose" (Freeman, 1984, p. 53). First introduced in the 1960s, the concept continues to generate interest in evaluating situations that involve competing interests. For instance, Jones and Wicks (1999) argue that "the interests of all (legitimate) stakeholders have intrinsic value, and no set of interests is assumed to dominate the others" (p. 207), while Jawahar and McLaughlin (2001) assert that at any given organizational life cycle phase, certain stakeholders will be more important than others. Regardless of which viewpoint you adopt, stakeholder theory can be adapted to describe the relative importance and legitimate claims of groups in the life cycle of the planning for, development of, and maintenance of campus physical learning spaces.

For purposes of this chapter, stakeholders are defined in Freeman's terms, as groups or individuals who can affect or are affected by the creation or use of physical learning spaces on the campus. Many groups have a stake in developing effective learning spaces. Figure 5.1 attempts to identify some of the most obvious, though not all may apply to every situation, list. As Figure 5.1 illustrates, students and faculty, as key users of the space, have an important stake in its development. Facilities managers, charged with facilitating the creation of the space and then maintaining it, have an agency role in the space, being agents for its creation and maintenance. Alumni have a stake in that the space provides them with nostalgic opportunities when they return to campus, and it offers them an opportunity to make donations to participate in the space's renovation or the creation of new space. State legislators, with fiduciary responsibilities and competing claims on state resources, have a stake in how resources are allocated to physical plants in state institutions. Every group identified in Figure 5.1 holds some claim to learning spaces, some more directly than others, and as the examples suggest, the claims can often be conflicting, as would be the contrast between faculty and students desiring productive workspaces with multiple features, and legislators desiring budget parsimony.

Table 5.1 looks in more detail at stakeholder groups that are critical to the development of innovative learning spaces. These groups, whose significant involvement is critical to designing learning spaces that will justify the existence of "brick and mortar" campuses (serving residential and commuter students) in the future, have vast differences in culture, perspective, and mind-set. Thus space design decision making has a strong potential for discord, which could yield suboptimal decisions. Each group has a different stake in the process of learning space creation or renovation, a traditional or typical level of involvement, limitations to effective involvement, a primary source of concern about the space, and a source of tension surrounding the process of learning space development. Table 5.1 captures these differences in an abbreviated way.

This description of campus fiefdoms may inadvertently leave the idea that these groups have irreconcilable differences and could never find a common ground or vision around which to coalesce. But collaborative structures and processes can be created by which these competing needs and interests can be harnessed to design and build learning environments that support learning without being inordinately difficult to maintain, finance, and sustain. The rich literature on cross-functional product development teams provides practical ideas that can shape the process by which useful learning spaces can be created on campuses. I turn now to this topic.

Factors in Creating Cross-Functional Learning Space Design Teams

New times call for new processes and structures and systems. . . . and new spaces. Higher education has been undergoing transformation and the new demands placed on it require serious thought on how to invest resources to support learning on (and off) campus. Other industries have faced transformational change sooner than higher education; their mistakes and successes can be instructive as higher education institutions try to navigate the white waters of collaborative work that this new era demands. It is important to change the way space is designed in order to harness its full potential in learning. The remainder of this chapter offers practical ideas to effect such change.

Table 5.1. Stakeholders Critical to Design of Learning Spaces Stakes, Levels of and Limitations to Involvement, Concerns and Tensions

Stakeholder group	Stake in process	Typical level of involvement	Limitations to effective involvement	Primary aspect(s) of concern about the space	Sources of tension over process
Faculty	Primary user	Low to moderate	Time, interest, and lack of awareness of importance of space design to learning	Space fits teaching style Space promotes learning Convenient	Dislike squelching debate in favor of efficiency
Students	Primary user	Low	Time and schedule often invisible to those making decisions	Accessibility and comfort Good learning attributes (acoustics, sight lines, work space for active involvement, etc.)	Dislike being patronized
Deans & other administrators	Responsible for managing the "real estate"	Low to moderate	Time and conflicting demands; expertise	Cost/value for investment Message space sends about quality of programs Student and faculty satisfaction	Dislike endless discussion without outcome
Student affairs/ development professionals	Advocates for student viewpoint; can be primary user when learning spaces in residential context	Low unless residential spaces	Sometimes not seen by academic side as campus resource; time	Focus on space that enhances student learning and growth Safety Mindful of role of out-of-the-classroom learning	Dislike being excluded
Disabilities professionals	Responsible for ensuring universal access	Consultative but often not involved deeply	Time; sometimes not consulted until after the fact	Universal access Logistics of making accommodations within a budget	Dislike being excluded
Facilities managers	Responsible for creating the "real estate"	High	Competing projects; time; logistical challenges	Make good decisions Efficiency Maintainability and durability Maintain good relationship with contractors Standardization and streamlining of complex processes	Dislike other stakeholders intruding into the technical domain and slowing or making more complicated or expensive the process
Architects	Responsible for designing and engineering the spaces	High	Competing projects; unclear direction as to what needed; need to move project to completion	Space makes a statement and enhances reputation, and generates more business	Dislike constraints on creative freedom and lack of committing sufficient resources to do the job "right"

Recognize the critical role of users and include them in the design process.
Faculty and students need to be more actively involved in shaping learning spaces in the future. Von Hippel (2001) has studied user innovation
communities, groups of innovators who band together to improve products or services they use, motivated by the desire to benefit from the
improvements. These groups, found in open-source software and even in
windsurfing gear, know exactly what they want and experiment with new
materials until a manufacturer copies their innovations and designs them
into the next generation of product. Although it would be foolish to think
that faculty and students know exactly what they want and have the technical expertise and capacity to design their own spaces, the current specialization of labor relegating the teaching and learning functions to faculty
and the design function to facilities managers is equally lacking.

Involving users in the design process can lead to extraordinary break-
throughs in thinking and design. Team New Zealand unexpectedly won the
America's Cup in 1995, demonstrating radical gains in boat speed. Their win
has been studied extensively and is a classic example of the power of involving users in decision making. They were able to beat their competitors not
because of superior technology but because of a process that gave them the
edge—and specifically, the fact that the users (sailors) were central to the
design. Maani and Benton (1999) offer this explanation: "To achieve a team-
oriented culture, traditional management structures were tipped upside
down, and the sailing team, who were the customers, were placed at the
pyramid's apex" (p. 57).

Do students and faculty sit at the pyramid's apex of designing spaces
for learning? Do they and their deans even recognize the critical role they
should play? Faculty and students are most aware of the limitations of a traditional classroom and are in the best position to experiment with new
forms or explore new ideas. Facilities managers, like manufacturers, cannot
know what users want as well as users themselves do. Faculty and students
must be critical and active participants in campus space design.

Create cross-functional design teams. The space development process
requires collaboration between academic and physical planners through
team-based project management. The process needs to be as broad and
inclusive as possible. As Anketell (1996) suggests, "attempts to scale down
the list [of participants] often lead to problems later which could result in
significant expense and delay. An open, inclusive process will strengthen
the constituent group's sense of ownership and will result in a successful
process and plan" (p. 120).

Who should participate in the lengthy, challenging, sometimes uncomfortable discussions required to transform traditional views of classroom
space use, guided by time-tested standards and rules, to new visions of
learning spaces? How will this group of individuals coalesce around a
shared vision, and how can they create a sense of community in which they
can have productive conversations that lead to team learning?

Research on effective collaboration and teamwork is plentiful (see, for example Hargrove, 1998; Manning, Curtis, and McMillen, 1996; and Schrage, 1995). Kets de Vries (1999) captures the characteristics of effective teamwork succinctly in his study of a very effective, team-oriented culture—the Pygmies. His work showed that members respect and trust each other, protect and support each other, engage in open dialogue and communication, share a strong common goal, have strong shared values and beliefs, subordinate their own objectives to those of the team, and subscribe to "distributed leadership," with roving leaders emerging at different times from within the team.

One could make the case that the set of qualities described in the preceding paragraph is a luxury that is afforded only to homogeneous teams, but effective multicultural teams have also been shown to exhibit the qualities Kets de Vries describes. Distefano and Maznevski (2000) studied multicultural teams and found that, compared to homogeneous teams, they can be more creative, generate more and better alternatives to problems, and generate more and better criteria for evaluating alternatives—all strong qualities for designing learning spaces. They found that the key to unlocking the creative synergy between the players was in their interaction processes—"how they understood, incorporated, and leveraged their differences" (p. 48), that is, worked to understand the differences rather than sweeping them under the rug and pretending they didn't exist.

In short, cross-functional design teams are more challenging than unilateral decision making but, managed properly, can lead to much better decision choices and much more valuable learning spaces being built.

Foster the development of leadership that can deal with significant differences in values and worldviews. Faculty, students, administrators, facilities managers, architects—all are necessary in the process of designing learning spaces, and all approach the task with different viewpoints, concerns, and values (see Table 5.1). How will leadership emerge to create a sense of common vision within this group of talented yet disparate individuals? What is needed is leadership that can deal with significant differences in values and worldview. It is essential that "the activity of people making sense and meaning of their work together becomes the source of leadership" (Drath, 2001, p. 10). Project Kaleidoscope, an NSF-funded organization that focuses on academic facilities design, calls for "project shepherds" for all building projects, faculty members from one of the departments that will locate within the new or renovated structure and who lead the effort (see http://spacesforlearning.udayton.edu). Conscious effort needs to be placed on working to make such leadership viable. Hierarchical models of maintaining the status quo, relying on traditional structures of organization, viewing self as specialist, ineffective listening or listening without willingness to abandon what one already believes, and attempts to control others by diminishing their talents must all be abandoned to make room for this newer way of interacting.

Recognize the importance of reward systems. People are unlikely to change their behavior or decision-making rules if their reward systems continue to reinforce the old behavior and rules. Expecting faculty to enthusiastically embrace their new charge as co-creators of learning spaces, without accounting for the added time and responsibility this will generate, is at best naive— and at worst, dangerous. They will need administrator support and recognition that the time they invest in the process will create results and that their efforts will be rewarded. Similarly, the assessment of facilities managers should be based on how well they enable learning, as well as on their efficiency and project completion.

Create experimental spaces for users to make new discoveries—and learn from them. When designing learning spaces on campuses, the opportunity to experiment (and fail) needs to be present. This means creating physical spaces where faculty can try out new teaching techniques (without fear that teaching evaluation ratings will drop) and new physical arrangements in the rooms. Creating some experimental learning spaces on campus, allowing faculty to apply to use them, and creating excitement around such spaces so that people will study the effects of their experiments on learning will enable faculty and students to increase knowledge of learning spaces. This can help guide the development of more permanent learning spaces in the future. The university would make more informed decisions and have a better sense of what would be valuable in subsequent building projects.

Align budget processes with learning space design initiatives. The degree to which learner-centered initiatives are adopted, and ultimately successful, depends on their acceptance as budget priorities (Anderes, 1996, p. 129). The integration of planning and budgeting for new space design is most likely to be successful when the process has active leadership and broad participation, translates planning priorities into budget initiatives, provides informational support to participants, adopts criteria and processes developed from within the team, provides ample opportunity for input and feedback on decisions to the communities served by the decision making, measures performance, and offers new funding models that share the risk of hybrid spaces with all relevant design team groups, rather than benefiting one group while creating unmanageable costs for another.

Slow down to speed up. In the rush to speed a construction or renovation project to completion, critical and fatal errors can be committed. Research on reducing product development lead times strongly cautions against rushing the design phase. Significant savings are achieved when design and process are improved early (Vesey, 1991), and failing to think through the programming expected in new learning spaces could cut off the possibility for true change. Designing new learning spaces is an innovative activity and requires participants to abandon their usual ways of interacting with each other, stop protecting their turf, and discover new ideas. Failing to invest adequate time in this process may result in spaces that are neither innovative nor appropriate for the future. The opportunity to build or renovate spaces happens infrequently; it is all the more important to avoid uninspired design, uninformed by the future realities of learning centeredness.

Harness the tension between creativity and the need for order. Shared knowledge, coordination and collaboration, and developing a shared vision have been highlighted as critical to effective design. These make collaborative inventiveness possible. Even though conversations between groups from very different worlds can be difficult at best, they are essential to arriving at a solution that makes sense (Brown and Duguid, 2001, p. 93). An inclusive process that involves the primary user community, that is, faculty and students, can generate new knowledge that transforms spaces. But that exploration of new ideas needs some structure that can transform the brainstorming ideas into real bricks and mortar; the groups traditionally associated with space design, architects and facilities managers, bring the requisite experience to emphasize this portion of the task. The process experts need to be willing to adapt their processes to the design needs of the teaching and learning experts, and the latter need to be willing to decide on a direction and move to implement it. The balance between these two forces is not easy to achieve (Brown and Duguid, 2001, p. 94):

Establishing processes emphasizes the hierarchical, explicit command-and-control side of organization—the structure that gets things done. By contrast, practice emphasizes the implicit coordination and exploration that produces things to do. Practice without process tends to become unmanageable; process without practice results in the loss of creativity needed for sustained innovation.

For successful projects to be created by a cross-functional learning space design team, the "creative abrasion" between the practice of exploring new learning space design possibilities and the standardized campus process for designing spaces need to meet somewhere in the middle; in essence, both need to be managed.

Conclusion

At the dawn of a new era for higher education and armed with much better understandings of how people learn, we have the opportunity to create and work in spaces that are much more conducive to learning than the spaces in which past generations were taught. The creation of such spaces calls for new ways of campus collaboration and the leaving behind of the specialist approach that consigned learning and teaching to faculty and students, design to campus specialists, and budgeting to financial officers. What is needed for the future is the development of collaborative skills and mindsets that will yield exciting and rejuvenating spaces that no one group could have conceived in isolation. Ultimately, leadership capability to foster and support new ways of interacting is critical.

References

Anderes, T. K. "Connecting Academic Plans to Budgeting: Key Conditions for Success." In B. Nedwek (ed.) *Doing Academic Planning: Effective Tools for Decision Making.* Ann Arbor, Mich.: Society for College and University Planners, 1996.

Anketell, D. "Integrating Academic and Facilities Planning." In B. Nedwek (ed.), *Doing Academic Planning: Effective Tools for Decision Making.* Ann Arbor, Mich.: Society for College and University Planners, 1996.

Brown, J. S., and Duguid, P. "Creativity vs. Structure: A Useful Tension" *Sloan Management Review,* 2001, 42(4), 93–94.

Distefano, J., and Maznevski, M. "Creating Value with Diverse Teams in Global Management." *Organizational Dynamics,* 2000, 29(1), 45–63.

Drath, W. "The Third Way: A New Source of Leadership." *Leadership in Action,* 2001, 21(2), 7–11.

Freeman, E. R. *Strategic Management.* Marshfield, Mass.: Pitman, 1984.

Hargrove, R. *Mastering the Art of Creative Collaboration.* New York: McGraw-Hill/Business Week Books, 1998.

Jawahar, I. M., and McLaughlin, G. L. "Toward a Descriptive Stakeholder Theory: An Organizational Life Cycle Approach." *Academy of Management Review,* 2001, 26(3), 397–414.

Jones, T. M., and Wicks, A. C. "Convergent Stakeholder Theory." *Academy of Management Review,* 1999, 24(2), 206–221.

Kets de Vries, M.F.R. "High Performance Teams: Lessons from the 'Pygmies,'" *Organizational Dynamics,* 1999, 27(3), 66–77.

Maani, K., and Benton, C. "Rapid Team Learning: Lessons from Team New Zealand America's Cup Campaign." *Organizational Dynamics,* 1999, 27(4), 48–62.

Manning, G., Curtis, K., and McMillen, S. *Building Community: The Human Side of Work.* Cincinatti, Ohio: Thomson Executive Press, 1996.

Project Kaleidoscope. Available online: http://spacesforlearning.udayton.edu.

Schrage, M. *No More Teams! Mastering the Dynamics of Creative Collaboration.* New York: Doubleday, 1995.

Vesey, J. "The New Competitors: They Think in Terms of 'Speed-to-Market.'" *Academy of Management Executive,* 1991, 5(2), 23–33.

Von Hippel, E. "Innovation by User Communities: Learning from Open-Source Software." *Sloan Management Review,* 2001 (Summer), pp. 82–86.

DEBORAH J. BICKFORD is associate provost for learnig, learning environments, and pedagogy, director of the Ryan C. Harris Learning Teaching Center, co-director of the Learning Village, and associate professor of management at the University of Dayton.

6

An architect explains the various planning steps necessary to create new spaces on campuses and reflects on characteristics of working relationships that are most effective in creating informed learning spaces.

Educator and Architect Partnerships for Success

James Butz

We've all experienced powerful environments that stimulate us physically, emotionally, and intellectually. It is easy to look at past masterpieces and think of the architectural creative genius. Creating architecture is a collaborative process involving architects, engineers, builders, financiers, facilities managers, and users. This collaboration resolves diverse requirements for budget, schedule, planning, zoning, codes, design vision, technical building details, mechanical and electrical performance, construction methodology, and building function. When the collaboration works well, buildings function efficiently, are affordable, contribute to our communities, and provide inspiring environments.

This collaboration has not reached its full potential in education—educators are important contributors but have not been as actively involved in the past and are novices to the process. When the ultimate users do not contribute and provide leadership, the architectural solution cannot be fully effective. This has never been as true as today in the midst of educational revolution. As education changes, so must the architecture that supports it. The architect can only understand this constantly evolving change through thoughtful interaction with educators.

This chapter explores the planning process and key considerations to a successful architectural collaboration. While the subject matter is too large to fully cover, this chapter provides a knowledge framework for educators to develop as they plan their facilities. It explores the planning participants, traditional planning process, and suggested changes in the planning process.

NEW DIRECTIONS FOR TEACHING AND LEARNING, no. 92, Winter 2002   © Wiley Periodicals, Inc.

Planning Participants

Of all the planning participants in a successful architectural project, three constituents are essential to a successful collaboration. Each has tremendous responsibilities to the team for communication, consensus building, and decision making. Each must make a personal commitment to the project and accept associated risks. These people are the primary user representative, the architect, and the facilities manager.

User Representative. The user representative is responsible for representing the extended user group, which includes students, administrators, faculty, and staff. This person must not only make sure that communication flows in both directions but that users actively contribute ideas, thoroughly evaluate information, and honestly express their opinions. The user representative should challenge the work and be an advocate for the internal functions of the building—explaining to the architect why user concerns are valid and explaining to the users why project constraints are real. More than anyone else, the user representative is the link between the design team and the occupants of the building. Good people and leadership skills are essential.

Architect. The architect represents the design team, which can number hundreds of professionals on large projects. Staff can include planners, architects, interior designers, cost estimators, construction administrators, and engineers for soils, structural, plumbing, mechanical, electrical, and technology systems. The primary architectural representative must work on several levels, from design visionary to technical detailer, from contract manager to consensus builder, and from engineering coordinator to cost estimator. Architects are artists who are willing to spend countless hours improving their designs. But architects must also be business professionals. They must manage consulting fees, control their risks, hold planning participants and contractors accountable, and inform clients when ideas are unrealistic. Architects are expected to design buildings that function well, protect public life and safety, withstand wear and tear, and are affordable and beautiful. Unlike manufactured products, buildings are expected to function perfectly upon completion, without the benefit of testing. Architects are therefore at risk from flawed details and unrealistic client expectations.

Facilities manager. The facilities manager manages the operational needs of the campus physical plant and promotes campus development. This person coordinates the efforts of campus planners, finance administrators, public safety officers, and managers for traffic, parking, utility infrastructure, campus grounds, and environmental health and safety. Facilities managers are liaisons between these various offices and academicians. They are responsible for implementing and conforming to institutionally adopted standards including master plans, project programming, design standards and community agreements. Facilities managers are responsible for managing the design process, specifically budgets, schedules, space allocation, quality expectations, and institutional risks. Because buildings are unique designs requiring millions of dollars, there is the constant risk of claims and lawsuits. The facilities manager must resolve such issues fairly and equitably. This part of architectural creation isn't glamorous, but it is as important as any other element.

Project Delivery Process

Architectural projects are typically conceived and implemented in six phases: programming, schematic design, design development, construction documents, bidding, and construction. Programming is the concept phase that describes intent. From this, owners make the go/no-go decision. Schematic design, design development, and construction documents compose a three-step process that begins with sketch studies and concludes with detailed technical documents. Each phase is more detailed and technical than the preceding one. The owner reviews, comments, and approves the design after each phase. Bidding is a transitional phase during which the design is put out for bid and construction contractors are awarded the work. Construction is the final phase, during which contractors have primary leadership responsibilities. The building is constructed, furniture and equipment is installed, and the user moves in. The following describes each phase in more detail.

Programming. The programming effort describes the requirements of the physical design in detail and results in a report called a "Program of Requirements." It states the owner's needs: activities to be housed, intended functions, vision statement, project goals, academic challenges, and development opportunities. The report establishes the development parameters of the project: building location, budget, schedule, and approval authority, and it describes space requirements by area allocation and room adjacencies. Detailed requirements for each space, building system, and site considerations are further articulated with words, data, diagrams, and photographs. The report typically describes the solution with words because the concept affects the programmatic results. However, the solution should not be designed at this phase so as to constrain the architect's creativity. This is an important and unconstrained opportunity for users to clearly communicate their expectations and needs with the design professionals prior to design decision making.

Schematic Design. Schematics is an interactive process between the design team and owner through which the optimum solution is created. The result is a site plan, floor plans, building sections, and exterior building elevations. The design is further described in outline specifications that describe building construction and mechanical and electrical systems. The construction cost is analyzed in further detail and necessary adjustments are made.

Design Development. During the design development phase, specific details of the construction are articulated, and all decisions for which the owner should have input are typically agreed upon.

Construction Documents. Preparation of the construction documents is the third and final design phase, during which the design team describes the conditions of the construction contracts in detail. Drawings are created for every construction trade. Detailed specifications are further developed, general conditions of the contract are described, and a final detailed estimate of cost is prepared.

Bidding. During the bidding phase, construction documents are distributed to prospective construction contractors for their use in preparing construction bids. Documents typically include technical drawings, written specifications for building materials and their installation, and legal contractual requirements to complete the work. The architect responds to bidders' questions and issues legally binding clarification documents called *addenda.* Bids are received, opened, and tabulated. The owner and architect evaluate the bids and the bidder's ability to perform. Preferred contractors are selected and contracts executed.

Construction. Contractors lead all construction activities and coordination between the trades. During this time, the architect administers the construction contracts. This includes observing the work for conformance with the construction documents, clarifying the intent of the construction documents, reviewing shop drawings, reviewing contractor applications for payment, responding to needed changes of the work, and documenting the progress of the work.

Overview of the Process. The project delivery process, from programming through construction, has several checkpoints to protect participants' interests. The user group has approval authority after programming to confirm that its needs have been completely and clearly documented. The user group has approval authority after each design phase to confirm that the design meets the program objectives. The facilities manager has approval authority after each programming and design phase to confirm the project is meeting budgetary and institutional development goals. The architect receives formal approvals of decisions upon which to base subsequent work. This process provides control, accountability, and efficiency.

The project delivery process develops from general ideas to specific details. The user group's input should be concentrated in the early phases. Design decisions requiring user group input should be completed by the end of the design development phase. Decisions made in the program, schematic, and design development phases have the greatest impact on design quality and budget conformance. By not understanding the process and their responsibilities, the users can unknowingly forfeit their input. Modifying decisions in later phases is tremendously challenging and expensive. The schedule can be jeopardized, commitments can be compromised, and the architect loses profitability.

In the absence of thoughtful user input, the facilities manager and architect are likely to base their work on past model solutions. For example, an educational facility can be a classroom building with a series of thirty-foot-square classrooms flanking each side of a corridor. Although this may have fit prevailing beliefs about appropriate pedagogy forty years ago, it won't necessarily work tomorrow. The influence of pedagogical shifts, technology integration, curriculum development, and the need for lifelong learning changes everything.

New environmental models will develop that haven't been conceived yet. Fundamental questions need to be asked that once were taken for granted. Who will be our students? How will we conduct class? How long will classes last? Should different functions be separated or fused? How much space should be allocated and shared? Who controls the space? How is student recruitment and retention being addressed? Will the new concept cost the same per square foot? Will the new concept require the same maintenance and energy costs? These questions are difficult to answer during a period of shifting paradigms, and will be even more difficult to predict for the next forty years. Yet these questions need to be answered by the planning participants in the context of use, design, and facilities management.

Suggestions for Enhancing Design Collaboration

To facilities managers and architects, the traditional project delivery process is fundamentally sound and well understood, but it is not ideal for the challenges faced today. In today's educational environment, the planning process should be more collaborative with educators because educators are on the front lines of attempting to focus on student learning. Collaboration should take place early in the project because it is during this period that user input is critical—how have space needs changed as we refocus our efforts from teaching to learning outcomes? The following suggestions are offered to enhance the personal relationship of the planning participants and thus, the effectiveness of their collaboration.

Designing a building typically becomes a personal mission for those directly involved because the result is a physical legacy that will have an impact on its community for generations. The design process is enhanced by personal relationships—mutual trust, shared commitments, and open communication. Understanding each other's individual interests is the foundation of a personal relationship. It is important for the participants to take time getting to know one another and to develop this relationship prior to commencing design. All participants should be realistic and open-minded during times of difficulties. Experimentation sometimes results in setbacks, and the team members have to trust one another to work through failed solutions to arrive at innovative ones.

Developing the project committee and clearly defining responsibilities and authority for each member are crucial for success. It is important to consider committee levels, that is, primary members and support members. Committee member ownership of the process is critical. They must be committed to the success of the project as well as be advocates for their constituency. The whole committee must understand that compromises will be made and that the committee members are responsible for shaping the best solution. All should rely on the individuals of the committee and design team staff. The primary representatives must focus on communication and team building, not micromanaging every detail.

Expanding the schedule of the project can allocate more time to programming and schematic design for careful consideration of issues and alternatives. Too often architects are hired with a time frame that demands immediate commencement of design, which bypasses important early conversation and team building. This schedule is often the result of not wanting to hire an architect until funding is in place. It is important to allocate funds for programming prior to design and construction. Allow time to fully develop the program for a limited financial risk.

Allocating time prior to formal programming to develop a shared understanding is valuable. Visit users' facilities and benchmarked programs at peer institutions. Review the design process and the importance of each step. Seek to frame the key questions without the pressure of answering them. Architecture is an educational process; treat it as such.

Hiring outside consultants to develop your program of requirements can bring fresh ideas to the institution, challenge old assumptions, and facilitate orderly decision-making.

Prior to hiring the architect, collaborate with the facilities manager to write the request for proposal for architectural services. When you buy a car, you start with a good idea of what's available and of the type and features you want. Yet many people select an architect without understanding the differences between firms or the services they offer. Campus facilities managers understand these differences and should consult with user representatives prior to requesting qualifications.

Some architectural firms have a general practice, serving all the needs of their client base. These firms can team with specialty firms, which are expert at design and aesthetics or specific project types. Some specialty firms also contract directly with institutions and can provide full services. They are often out-of-town firms that have developed their operations to practice across long distances. However, they have difficulty being as responsive as in-town firms are during the construction documents, bidding, and construction phases.

Firms that specialize in learning environments understand the issues facing educators. They have experience in understanding the nuances of specific programs and can more readily interpret them into new concepts. Trust and consensus are built earlier in the design process.

Architectural firms offer a wide array of services. The American Institute of Architects (AIA) has developed standard agreements that are understood in the industry. Many institutions have standard agreements modeled after AIA agreements. They define the services and performance of the parties. Generally, architectural services are described as basic and additional. Basic are the minimum services to design, bid, and administer construction. They exclude programming, exhaustive studies, renderings, models, and full-time construction representation. These services are just a few of the additional services architects can provide. The more comprehensive the services negotiated, the more responsive the architect can be to the user's needs. More fees are required with more services, which takes away from capital improvements. The fee spent to expand services during programming and schematic design is important in defining viable solutions for tomorrow's learning environments.

The architect should have an appreciation for the educational change occurring and have a desire to develop a thorough understanding of the user's activities and needs before commencing design. The architect should recognize that the building is being designed for how learning will occur in the future, not how it has been constrained by past philosophies and building design. Developing this understanding requires time and exploratory conversation. This is the opportunity for educators to contribute expertise by explaining learning processes and identifying educational challenges.

User representatives should embrace the contractual relationship between the architect and institution. The architect has legal obligations to perform, all of which require time and money. Large fees negotiated with architects often yield 5 percent profit or less. Excessive effort spent in any one area limits the architect's effectiveness in other tasks. Often the user group isn't involved with the architectural contract, even though it dictates what services will be provided.

Users should be encouraged to participate in the negotiation process for architectural services. Understand what services are available, and what the cost and value is. Help select those services that will benefit the project. Besides the extra services mentioned in connection with the basic agreement (programming, exhaustive studies, renderings, models, and full-time construction representation) architects can also provide benchmarking trips, specialty design expertise, community presentations, and procurement of furnishings and technology.

Users should also be encouraged to participate in developing the work plan. Understand when decisions need to be made and communicate what is necessary for the users to make such decisions.

Establish a shared vocabulary with the facilities managers and architects. Words are powerful but can mean different things to different people. A *learning environment* to an educator could be the people and technology, but to an architect the term means bricks and mortar.

Architectural terminology can be intimidating to anyone not in the business. This is particularly threatening to educators, who are used to being the holders of knowledge. The same observation is true for educational terminology and its effect on architects who specialize in educational facilities. Planning participants should feel comfortable enough in their relationship to say, "*I don't understand.*" The consequence of not expressing confusion is design development based on misinformation.

Everyday terminology establishes mental pictures that we often don't question. For example, a classroom has come to be thought of as the place where education occurs. It is a thirty-foot square room with rows of desks and an instructor in front. Developing new names causes planning participants to challenge solutions and to see spaces in a different light. How might a studio be configured to house mathematics classes?

Architects think graphically. When communicating with architects, it might be helpful to use videos, photographs, and sketches to discuss your functions or ideas you've come across in other buildings. Storyboards and picture books can help create collages of thoughts. Use all means available to supplement your description of what you want to be able to do, but don't fall into the trap of trying to design the solution. The user responsibility is to define need and evaluate if the architect's solution will work.

Learn how to work effectively with architects and facilities managers before commencing large and complex projects. Start with a simpler project such as a classroom renovation, where the stakes are relatively low. The tasks are practically the same as for a new building. The primary difference is the number of people on the team. By completing such a project, the user representative is able to create a how-to guide. This enables the user representative to refine the process and to counsel members of the larger committee in fulfilling their responsibilities.

Approach your building as an experiment. Buildings are often designed for one group of individuals but used by different people. Retirement, career moves, and the building life cycle all contribute. To think every detail will be perfect for forty years is unrealistic. The building must adapt as well as the users.

In facilitating the transformation to learning-centeredness, the details alone don't define success. What do are the program concept, spatial environment, design character, and building flexibility. New solutions for these concerns will emerge through experimentation and evaluation. Each new solution will enable educators to do things unimaginable today, which will cause a reaction by the building, which will cause the next round of evolution. In each phase of this evolution, there will be successes and failures, but learning will always occur. Constant modifications to a building will probably be a marker for educational success.

It is wise to seek a partnership with the facilities manager and architect to periodically evaluate building performance and to make recommendations for short-term solutions. Applying these lessons to future improvements in the building and to new projects across campus is imperative to campus learning.

You can find interesting concept solutions outside of academic designs. For example, retail and residential buildings offer ideas for social interaction areas. Experimenting on paper and in existing facilities with translating these ideas to facilitate learning and maintaining ongoing dialogue with your architect and facilities manager are useful activities in driving continuous learning.

Function and budget should guide all decisions. The form wants to follow the function, so if the function is radically different, so will be the form. The best solution may not look like a traditional academic building in appearance, materials, or construction. A new idea that challenges today's standard sometimes becomes tomorrow's standard. The architectural solution must be more than a concept. It must be developed so it stands the test of time. The collaborative relationship of team members must be strong enough to allow them to thoroughly challenge each other, to demand the design will work in all aspects.

Strive to exhilarate people. Thousands, if not millions, of decisions are made in the course of an architectural project. Most of them are mundane and spread out over years. Projects can become drudgery if people aren't inspired. It helps to set a bold vision that challenges people every day to perform above their capabilities.

Responding to people's emotions is part of an effective process. The user groups should be challenging themselves to create the benchmark learning environment. The architects should be challenging themselves to create powerful physical environments and to create art through architecture. Together, the efforts of all should be focused on creating a masterpiece that will be admired for generations.

An important step is to define the outcome of the project, and by doing so define the essence of success. Thinking without constraints can clarify the big picture. Seeking input from all concerned parties is imperative for success, but it is important to recognize that the project won't be able to accommodate all interests. In the end, the vision must be bold, clear, and represent a voice of the leadership. The solution will be bold, clear, and an artistic statement of the architect's interpretation of the project's vision, discerned from the voices of the user groups.

Embrace the concept of modeling results in honest dialogue and open-mindedness. We all have vocabularies that are powerful to us but have little meaning to others. Visualization of concepts creates understanding, and alternative concepts place higher priorities on different project elements. The debate to determine the preferred solution resolves conflict and invariably ends in the creation of a new concept that meets the project's criteria for success.

Creating architecture creates professional and financial risks. Typically, the more innovative solutions have more risks. Many people don't care to acknowledge or deal with this, which can cause planning participants to become untrusting and divided.

A safe and traditional architectural solution may not facilitate educational evolution, and it will certainly constrain the next generation of educators. The most appropriate architectural solution may be very unusual for a campus, thus open to criticism. An innovative solution may not initially function completely as intended, thus requiring additional work to perfect. This can be viewed either as a failure or as research and development for the institution.

The users are at risk of receiving a building that doesn't meet their future needs. The facilities manager is at risk of a project that requires unavailable time and money to modify. And the architect is at financial risk in developing innovative solutions for traditional fees. The user representative, facilities manager, and architect should encourage each other to jointly manage their risks through open communication, consensus building, testing of ideas, and work plan management. Take sufficient time in early phases to fully explore ideas.

The user representative should be encouraged to research the institution's adopted design guidelines and consult with the facilities manager and architect as to their interpretation. These guidelines may include a campus master plan, a technology master plan, and space management standards, design standards, and standard details and specifications. These guidelines can dictate design decisions as well as make accommodations for specific project requirements. The planning participants should discuss the reasons behind such standards and jointly decide when to deviate from them.

Conclusion

Collaboration requires a commitment from each of the primary partners to one another's mutual success and to a shared definition of project success. Collaboration is based on personal relationships, not contractual responsibility. These relationships need to be developed early in the programming process where key irreversible decisions are made. This investment of time and energy will pay off with saved efforts in later phases and solutions that meet the educator's requirements.

JAMES BUTZ, AIA, is chief architect of Burgess & Niple, Ltd.; he operates out of the firm's Columbus, Ohio, office.

7

This chapter focuses on the process used at one university for developing a long-term vision and implementation plan for the renovation and refurbishment of existing classroom space.

Developing a Classroom Vision and Implementation Plan

Julia Christensen Hughes

Increased attention is being placed on campus learning spaces, attributable to several factors including the general age and condition of campus classrooms, renewed interest in infrastructure investment, the introduction of advanced learning technologies, a shift in pedagogy from faculty-centered to student-centered, and a growing recognition of the important role that classroom and other learning environments play in student learning and retention.

Wilke (2000), citing college-level outcome-based research by DeYoung (1977), Fraser and Treagust (1986), and Vahala and Winston (1994), concluded that a positive classroom learning environment can result in "higher levels of involvement, personalization, student cohesiveness, task orientation, innovation, and individualization" (p. 9) as well as have a significant impact on attendance, satisfaction with the course and its content, and final course grades. The physical design of the classroom and the selection of its contents can play a significant role in shaping this environment and the pedagogy that is used within it.

In keeping with this view, interest is growing in a variety of classroom attributes such as movable tables and chairs that can accommodate group work, sight lines that encourage class discussion; aisles or other sufficient

I would like to acknowledge the tremendous support and contributions of Steve Borho, Ruth Gillespie, Jody Hendry, George Taylor, and Susan Rimkus of TSS along with all members of the Classroom Advisory Committee during various stages of this project. Thanks also to Chris Pickard of Physical Resources for his helpful comments on an earlier draft of this chapter.

space to allow the teacher to circulate easily among students, and movable podiums that avoid the creation of physical and symbolic barriers between student and teacher. There is also increased demand for new learning technologies such as classroom data projectors, computers, and connectivity.

Accommodating these needs is not easy. Financial, organizational, and attitudinal barriers abound: many universities are facing declining operating budgets; classrooms are typically supported by disparate departments; and the design of new classrooms often lacks a pedagogical focus. Tanner (2000) observed that school and classroom construction often lacks vision and that architectural considerations are rarely informed by pedagogy; "communications barely exist between the research branches of education and architecture" (p. 311).

These factors require those who support various aspects of campus classrooms to come together with those who support pedagogy and faculty development to challenge outdated classroom ideas and design approaches, and to develop common visions along with new organizing systems and structures. This process occurred in the late 1990s at the University of Guelph, a comprehensive university in southern Ontario, Canada, with approximately fifteen thousand students organized into six colleges, and a hundred centrally controlled and supported classrooms. This chapter provides an overview of the planning approach taken at the university in response to the opportunity for reinvestment in its classrooms.

The Context

Opportunities for change at the University of Guelph came from several directions. Of note, in 1995 the university formally adopted "learner-centeredness" as one of its strategic directions. It also formally acknowledged that more support was needed for the effective use of learning technologies. At about the same time, however, student enrollments were increasing and government operating grants, the key source of revenue for Ontario universities, were being reduced.

The Planning Process

In 1997, Teaching Support Services (TSS), an academic support unit with responsibility for classroom design, repair and maintenance of classroom audiovisual equipment, curriculum development support, training in the effective use of learning technologies, and providing resources and educational opportunities for faculty and TAs on a wide variety of pedagogical issues, brought attention to the condition of the classrooms and the need to reinvest in them. In 1999 TSS obtained $400,000 from central administration for classroom reinvestment. Committed to ensuring that this investment would contribute to a well-integrated, long-term classroom plan, TSS formed the Classroom Advisory and Planning Committee, which was made up of faculty representatives from each of the university's six colleges, experts in pedagogy and classroom design from Teaching Support Services, and support staff from a variety of departments including Physical Resources (which was responsible for mechanical, electrical, decorating, custodial services, architectural plans, and construction and renovation); Computing and Communications Services (which was responsible for the installation and maintenance of the campus communications infrastructure); and the Office of Registrarial Services (which was responsible for course and room scheduling).

The committee developed the following mandate:

Develop a long-term vision and multi-staged implementation plan for classroom reinvestment at the University of Guelph.
Establish short-term priorities to direct the investment of $400,000 by February 1999.

Once the mandate was determined, the group brainstormed a draft list of guiding principles to serve as a vision for the planning process. The principles were based on the classroom design literature as well as the experience of members of the planning group and included such attributes as "pedagogical flexibility," and "technological consistency."

Next, a classroom survey was designed and distributed to all faculty, receiving a response rate of 29.6 percent (247/835). A modified survey was also sent to a group of student leaders, who had a response rate of 26 percent (39/150). Other data were collected through conversations between faculty and their college representatives, a tour of selected campus classrooms, and a review of a recently updated classroom inventory.

Survey Results

Faculty were asked if they were in agreement with the draft guiding principles and to make suggestions for their improvement. The respondents were almost unanimous in their support (99 percent). They were also asked to indicate the importance of a variety of classroom technologies, for four sizes of classrooms (up to forty seats, forty-one to sixty seats, sixty-one to eighty seats, and more than eighty-one seats). Although the results varied somewhat between the colleges, they were surprisingly consistent across room sizes, providing support for the principle of technological consistency.

Technologies that were rated as being either somewhat or extremely important, across all class sizes, by the majority of respondents from all six colleges included chalkboard, overhead projector, computer monitor, and computer projector. For classes of eighty or more, a computer interface, sound system, and wireless microphone were also rated as being important.

Technologies that were rated as being either somewhat or extremely important, across all room sizes, by the majority of respondents from some but not all six colleges, included computer interface (five colleges); video-tape recorder (four colleges); slide projector (four colleges); computer (three colleges); white board (two colleges); and network connection (one college).

The technology that was seen as being not at all important by the majority of respondents was the document camera, followed by network connection and white board. We wondered to what extent these responses reflected a lack of access to or familiarity with these technologies versus an informed opinion.

Faculty were also asked to indicate the importance of a number of classroom features. Within this category there was considerably more variation by college and by class size. However, a number of general observations can be made. For example, the majority of respondents across all colleges and class sizes thought having a movable podium was somewhat or extremely important. This is counter to the trend on many campuses of building large fixed podiums, which are used to store and control a myriad learning technologies. Other observations included:

- Movable chairs and tables were considered somewhat or extremely important in the smaller class sizes in all colleges except one.
- A center aisle was considered important by respondents from all colleges, but responses varied as to what class size requires it (forty, sixty, or eighty seats).
- Tiered seating was considered important by respondents from all colleges, but once again varied by class size (forty or sixty seats).
- Horseshoe seating was supported by the majority of colleges at various class sizes (less than forty, forty, or sixty).
- Telephones were considered important by respondents from the majority of colleges at various class sizes (forty-plus, sixty-plus, eighty-plus, all).
- Tablet arms were considered important by respondents from all colleges, for the majority of class sizes. Bench tables were not.

This final result was not expected, given anecdotal evidence that faculty were frustrated by classroom furniture that did not support collaborative group work. Furthermore, tablet arms provide limited desk space, which can restrict the use of student laptops and can also result in cramped conditions for writing examinations. Written comments, as well as responses to the open-ended question at the end of the survey, suggested that faculty may have had difficulty interpreting this question. Some faculty thought they were being asked, "Do you want tablet arms or no writing space at all?" Others indicated that they didn't know what bench tables were.

Next, faculty and students were asked to indicate the relative importance for several potential investment areas. They were told that their

Table 7.1. Investment Priorities for Faculty and Students

Investment Area	Faculty Mean Score (1 = not at all important, 5 = extremely important)	Student Mean Score (1 = not at all important, 5 = extremely important)
Upgrading classroom equipment	4.38	4.36
Upgrading classroom furniture (tables, chairs, curtains)	3.79	4.13
Improving classroom layout (seating, number of seats, sight lines, faculty space)	3.61	4.08
Improving lighting and lighting controls	3.52	3.72
Upgrading the physical plant (heating or cooling, ventilation, painting, floor, ceiling, walls)	3.42	4.18
Installing network connectivity (where absent)	2.93	2.84
Improving access and security	2.68	3.15

responses would help establish priorities. Means for each area are provided in Table 7.1. For both students and faculty, upgrading classroom equipment and furniture were particularly important, whereas installing network connectivity and dealing with room access and security were less so. In contrast, upgrading the physical plant was the second most important area for the students, while it was only the fifth most important for faculty.

Faculty offered many comments in response to the open-ended question at the end of the survey. They were invited to elaborate on their classroom design and equipment needs as well as mention issues associated with specific classrooms. The comments included requests for the following:

- More and better-equipped seminar rooms (ten to forty seats) and large lecture theaters (more than three hundred seats)
- More flexibility in classroom layout (movable tables and chairs)
- Better-designed classrooms (for visual and auditory needs)
- Resolution of basic issues (cleanliness, broken equipment and furniture, poor light controls, walls in need of paint)
- A reduction in the number of seats in some rooms
- Better air quality and in-room temperature controls
- Better quality and availability of projection equipment (need for two screens)
- More left-handed seating
- Clocks
- Computer technology and connectivity

Comments were also made on specific classrooms. Several pertained to classrooms in one particular building, where classrooms were referred to as "like an inner city building" and "a disaster area!" Faculty complained about the heavy furniture, the poor ventilation system, and the overcrowding.

The students also offered many comments. While many were similar to those raised by the faculty, there were some interesting differences. For example, there were many more comments on the lack of left-handed seats, along with the observation that with bench tables this would not be an issue. There were also several comments on broken, wobbly, and uncomfortable chairs. Interestingly, students also wrote about the need for faculty to receive training in classroom technology, including the use of overhead projectors and light controls. Finally, one student wrote passionately about the need to deal with basic issues before making major investments in learning technologies:

> Surely classrooms with the most basic needs unfulfilled should be considered before classrooms are hooked up to an analog phone line. . . . For example. . . . [the Fine Art building] is in need of a better ventilation system as students are working around toxic materials. [It] is [also] in need of chairs, plain old-fashioned chairs. Yes, most Fine Art students endure 3-hour lectures supported by tiny metal stools after the limited chairs with backs have been fought over.

Overview and Explanation of the Recommendations Generated

The results were reviewed by the Classroom Advisory and Planning Committee. A follow-up campus tour confirmed the particularly deplorable state of many of the classrooms that were specifically named. Broken chairs stacked in corners, water-damaged and badly stained carpets, cracked walls and peeling paint, and immovably heavy furniture were found to be quite common in one building and helped to identify classrooms in most need of a substantial overhaul. Other issues were identified through discussions among the committee's support department representatives with respect to operational challenges.

These findings led to the development of a series of recommendations, which were incorporated into a report and presented to the Vice President's Advisory Committee. The first recommendation dealt with the long-term vision. The original guiding principles were amended to place increased emphasis on physical plant conditions. The report provided justification for each principle, and in some cases, subsidiary recommendations were made. These are summarized in Table 7.2 and include pedagogical flexibility, technological consistency, simplicity of design and support for use of classroom equipment, reliability and durability of furniture and ongoing maintenance for it, accessibility and security of rooms and equipment, and minimum standards of the physical plant.

Table 7.2. Summary of Recommended Guiding Principles

Principle	Explanation	Importance and Outcomes	Examples
Pedagogical flexibility	To accommodate a variety of active learning and teaching approaches.	To support learner-centeredness, faculty pedagogical preferences, and examinations.	Movable bench tables and chairs; conduit in floor channels to accommodate student laptops in a variety of locations; variety of learning technologies; horseshoe layouts when fixed seating required; double rows in tiered classrooms.
Technological consistency	Development and implementation of a learning technology standard (type of equipment and brand).	Faculty confidence in equipment availability and function (ease of use); equality of access; simplified room scheduling; efficiencies in purchase, repair, and maintenance.	All rooms to have a minimum of chalkboard or white board; document camera; screen; data and video projector; videotape recorder; computer interface; faculty network connection; clock; telephone. Same brands and models to be used wherever possible.
Simplicity and support	Ease of use by faculty to be a significant determinant in the equipment brand standard. Training materials and support to be readily available.	To support the effective use of learning technologies by faculty and to build faculty confidence.	Clearly marked and easily manipulated controls; development of enhanced instructions; online training materials; one-on-one and group-based training sessions at the beginning of each semester.
Reliability and durability; ongoing maintenance and replacement	Reliability, durability, and ease of maintenance to be significant determinants in the equipment brand standard and furnishings selected. Operating budget to be provided for timely repair or replacement of damaged and obsolete equipment.	To maximize life of investment; prevent disruptions to teaching; minimize labor required for maintenance purposes; support planning for equipment replacement and upgrade.	Reliability and durability to be major considerations in purchase decisions. Secure an operating budget to provide for maintenance and repair, including equipment parts (such as bulbs for data projectors), as well as for the timely upgrade and replacement of equipment.
Accessibility and security (room and equipment)	Ensure accommodation and access to classrooms and classroom equipment for faculty, students, and support staff. Ensure security of equipment.	To provide timely access to classrooms; to accommodate students and faculty with physical disabilities or left-handedness; to provide security for classroom investments.command.	Clarify responsibility for room and equipment security; develop processes and implement systems to improve service and security; implement automatic classroom scheduling system and give service providers online access to room availability information; use bench tables to accommodate left-handed students; use electronic podiums (automatic lift switch) to support faculty of different heights (including wheelchair use); assign a variety of seating areas for students using wheelchairs.
Minimum standards for physical plant	All classrooms to at least meet minimal standards pertaining to condition of wall coverings and carpeting, cleanliness, furniture availability and condition, lighting, air quality, and appropriate temperatures.	To ensure a comfortable and effective learning and teaching environment.	Establish standards (frequency and type of housekeeping and painting, air quality, in-room temperature controls, condition of furniture and carpeting); assess current condition of all classrooms against these standards; develop plan for dealing with variances.

Following these recommendations, the report offered suggestions that dealt with potential barriers and operational issues. For example, it discussed the need to provide adequate base funding, to assign coordinating responsibility for the classrooms, to establish an automated classroom management system (to track complaints and work orders and to provide updated information on room attributes); and to establish a planning process for the ongoing prioritization of minor classroom improvements as well as comprehensive upgrades.

With respect to the current investment of $400,000, the report suggested that a three-pronged approach be taken: fix or upgrade minor equipment, furniture, layout, and physical plant issues in classrooms across campus ($90,000), increase the availability of classroom technology ($60,000), and undertake a comprehensive upgrade of several classrooms (5 @ $50,000 = $250,000). It was also felt that this general framework should continue to inform future reinvestments. In identifying the classrooms that would receive a comprehensive upgrade, several factors were taken into consideration. It was recommended that we upgrade a block of classrooms (for efficiency of installation and maximum visual impact) that were in poor condition, in high demand, and used by faculty and students from several departments and colleges.

The report was well received by the Vice President's Advisory Council. The short-term investment plan was approved, and CTS was acknowledged as the appropriate coordinator for managing the project and, in collaboration with the other support departments, became responsible for making progress on the other issues raised. Funds were also made available to support the development of an automated classroom management system.

The Picture Today

The planning process and the recommendations it generated proved pivotal in helping the university understand and address both its short-term and long-term classroom needs. Progress was also made on some of the longer-term recommendations. For example, a comprehensive classroom standard was developed and a master list of classroom renovation priorities was created, which is now updated on an annual basis. With these two documents in hand, when additional funding did become available in 2001, Guelph was able to put the projects in motion relatively quickly.

Perhaps most significantly, however, the classroom project served to raise awareness about the range of issues that need to be considered when constructing and maintaining effective learning spaces. This impact was timely. As a result of a new provincial government program—SuperBuild—the University of Guelph is now in the process of constructing one large classroom complex on its Guelph campus and another with a partner institution (Humber College) in Toronto. Members of the newly created Classroom Planning and Operations Committee (an offshoot of the Advisory and Planning Committee) were invited to participate in the selection and ongoing work of the architects for both of these projects, bringing increased attention to pedagogical and maintenance considerations. In both instances the guiding principles and classroom standards were instrumental. Without these documents and the conviction of the people involved, some of the principles might have been compromised in response to ever-present budgetary pressures.

Another government program—Facilities Renewal—has significantly increased the university's ability to renovate and refurbish existing space. Six million dollars will be invested in renovation activity on the Guelph campus in the coming year, and more funds are likely to be available in the future. Once again, the work of the Classroom Advisory and Planning Committee proved instrumental in directing this work.

Implications and Conclusions

Several observations can be drawn from Guelph's experience that may have implications for others. Given that these observations are based on the experience of just one university, they should necessarily be treated as tentative in nature.

Vision and guiding principles. Guiding principles should be developed that help direct the development of learning spaces on a long-term basis. These principles should be strongly linked to pedagogical theory and the strategic directions and priorities of the institution.

Leadership and structure. The design and maintenance of effective learning spaces requires effective leadership; people who are committed to effective pedagogy and have the support of senior administration. An effective organizing structure—like the Classroom Planning and Operations Committee—with representation from all those departments that play a role in supporting campus classrooms is needed.

Faculty and student input. Mechanisms should be developed that provide faculty, students, and program committees with the opportunity to give input into classroom design and technology selection. Ideally, these opinions will not only reflect current practice and preferences but will also take into account technological innovation and anticipated curricular changes.

Classroom inventory. A comprehensive list of all learning spaces along with room and technology attributes, and an assessment of the condition of each, should be developed and regularly updated. Such a list can prove essential in helping direct renovation and refurbishment projects and for matching faculty pedagogical preferences with assigned teaching space. Automating this inventory can help track repair and maintenance work.

Achieving balance. Reinvestment in learning spaces should balance the need to adopt new learning technologies with the need to ensure at least minimal standards of physical plant and room attributes. Minor upgrades, technology enhancements, and comprehensive upgrades should all be addressed as part of any reinvestment program.

Having implemented most of these guidelines, Guelph was well prepared to deal with the opportunities that it was presented with in 2001. The university is now in the process of revisiting these past accomplishments so that continuous improvement can be achieved.

References

DeYoung, A. "Classroom Climate and Class Success: A Case Study at the University Level." *Journal of Educational Research,* 1977, *70*(5), 252–256.

Fraser, B. J., and Treagust, C. F. "Validity and Use of an Instrument for Assessing Classroom Psychosocial Environment in Higher Education. *Journal of Higher Education,* 1986, *15,* 37–57.

Tanner, C. K. "The Influence of School Architecture on Academic Achievement." *Journal of Educational Administration,* 2000, *38*(4), 309–330.

Vahala, M. E., and Winston, R. B., Jr. "College Classroom Environments: Disciplinary and Institutional-Type Differences and Effects on Academic Achievement in Introductory Courses." *Innovative Higher Education,* 1994, *19,* 99–122.

Wilke, C. J. "Preferred College Classroom Environment Scale: Creating Positive Classroom Environments." *Journal of the First-Year Experience,* 2000, *12*(2), 7–32.

JULIA CHRISTENSEN HUGHES *is director of teaching support services and associate professor in the School of Hotel and Food Administration at the University of Guelph.*

Outdated classrooms are common in higher education.
This chapter unveils the story of what resulted when a
college's new focus on teaching led to tackling its
outmoded classroom inventory.

Put Your Money Where Your Mouth Is: A Case Study

Joan DeGuire North

The phrase "put your money where your mouth is" took on new meaning when ten years ago our college identified a focus on teaching as its top priority.

The College of Professional Studies (CPS) is one of four colleges at the University of Wisconsin–Stevens Point, an eight-thousand-student campus in the snowy center of Wisconsin. CPS contains various professional schools such as education; communicative disorders; health, exercise science, and athletics; health promotion and human development; medical technology; and interior architecture. We are a typical Carnegie Classification I university with the historic mantle of a teacher's college. Over the years, like so many of our type, we had aspired to greatness, which often meant establishing a reputation for research and grants. And we had done well, but faculty in my college began to point out the many ways that the university in general and I as its dean were putting less emphasis on teaching and learning. I discovered much to my chagrin that they were right, so in 1992 we created a "Focus on Teaching" priority that has remained a cornerstone of our culture.

With our eyes now focused on teaching, it was not long before someone cynically commented on the contrast between our two carpeted conference rooms, with wood tables and chairs, and our classrooms, which had vintage linoleum floors, plastic tablet chairs of many hues all in rows, and original paint. There was no escape from the impression that our meetings were more important than our classes. So in 1994 the CPS department heads made the historic decision to forgo receiving additional budget allocations from year-end funds for their individual departments. Instead, they decided to direct some or all of the college discretionary funds toward improving the learning environments of the college class-rooms. They made that decision seven years in a row.

Thus began our excursion into the world of classroom design. Now, after seven years, all classrooms in the college have been renovated with an eye toward making them more learning-focused, more conducive to classroom discussion, small groups, and frequent interactions—and inex-pensively. Additions included carpeting, tables, upholstered chairs, paint, thin-coat plaster viewing surfaces, and multiple white boards. Many classrooms have also been equipped with ceiling projectors, video pre-sentation displays (called "elmos"), and computers. Our Web site dis-plays a detailed listing of equipment and room layout. A link to the site is available at http://spacesforlearning.udayton.edu. About $200,000 (or 7 percent of our yearly budget) in college funds (and additional help from state grants) has been used over the past seven years for these ren-ovations. Since we have created such a comprehensive classroom makeover in a relatively few years, without significant outside funds, our story might be useful to others.

Who Owns the Classrooms?

Nothing at all had been done in the classrooms since they were first created some thirty years earlier, so our first struggle was to unearth whoever was responsible for classrooms. Did we have to ask permission to renovate and if so, from whom? Were there guidelines? No one seemed to know. Classrooms seemed to get born and live forever without need for any centralized campus life support. Faculty thought someone "upstairs" was responsible, but facili-ties offices on campus said, "Not us." No wonder our 1960s look lingered so long. So we set off on our own.

Multiple departments in the college use most of the classrooms in the college's two buildings, so we placed coordination for the upgrades in my lap. Going from no one being responsible for classrooms to the Dean's Office being responsible began the transformation. There seem to be sev-eral advantages to college-level coordination. Since none of us were ren-ovation experts, it made sense for one person to study, experiment, and learn about classroom design rather than leaving each department to go its own way. We aimed for different designs based on pedagogical differ-ences, economies of scale, and a compatible look for classrooms fronting the same hallway. The college "cabinet"—department heads and dean—determined the priority sequence of renovations and went money-in-hand to request a place on the building repair schedule. Handling the renova-tions within the college increased the sense of ownership and allowed us to design the rooms according to the teaching situations most character-istic of our college.

Changes We Made

Working with groups of interior design students (conveniently located in the college), we surveyed both students and faculty, asking them what changes in their classrooms might better facilitate student learning. In the beginning our student researchers interviewed students and faculty as they left classes; later the interviews moved to more formal surveys. In general, the faculty and students wanted classrooms that helped students participate actively in classes, provided better access to technology, and provided a more comfortable learning setting.

Oust the tablet chairs. The strongest recommendation was to replace plastic tablet chairs with tables and chairs. Students had complained about discomfort and, in some cases, not being able to fit into the small space between the tablet and chair. Students associated tablet chairs with children's class space and suggested that they did not feel treated as adults while trapped in "kiddie" chairs. Faculty members noted the structure of the tablet chair psychologically isolated students from each other with the tablet providing distance from others. They argued that tables with several chairs automatically created a learning community, small group for discussion, or, at the very least, a place where students belonged with other students. Faculty also mentioned that they preferred their classroom space to be equipped with furniture that could be used flexibly, moved to a circle or several groups or whatever would best support the pedagogy, so the new tables and chairs should not be affixed to the floor. Last, tablet chairs had often ended up in mixed colors in rooms, providing an unsettling discordant feeling from the lack of aesthetics. The new chairs were one common color. Chairs and tables were often the most expensive items in a renovation, so we sought bulk discounts (reminding sales staffs that we would be coming back for more orders for years to come). We stuck with one company and bought simple models with few or no moving parts. We also used some secondhand tables that had been relaminated by a company in town. At one point a furniture company discounted its merchandise price and took a charitable gift deduction.

Carpet the floors. The next most desired change was substituting carpeting for linoleum on the floors. In many cases, we chose the more expensive carpet tiles rather than the less expensive rolled carpet because rolled carpet required that we remove our linoleum tiles, an expensive process involving asbestos abatement. Carpet tiles are also easier to replace. In many cases, we had enough carpet tiles left over to carpet faculty offices, even if we had to create patterns on the floor from different carpet tiles.

Both students and faculty noted how much easier it was to hear each other on carpeted floors. Carpeting made the rooms seem more inviting and casual, leading some staff to suggest that the carpeting had a positive impact on student attitude and willingness to talk. For teaching applications where sitting on the floor might be warranted, carpeting certainly was more conducive to cooperation.

Put in white boards. The jury is still out, but initially there was strong sentiment for replacing chalk blackboards with white boards because they provided more opportunity for visual clues with color markers and easier reading from the white surface. Erasures from the blackboards created a dust that some people found irritating and the erasures themselves were never complete. We chose to keep the old blackboards, avoiding the extra cost for taking them down; instead we simply added whiteboards to the "back" wall and reversed the rooms. Now, between the new white boards and the old blackboards, there is ample space for multiple group reports on boards. Always scanning for economical renovation, however, we made the mistake of buying less expensive white boards that would not erase after several days' usage. Now there is dry eraser wall paper available.

Upgrade the technology. By most standards our college was fairly sophisticated with vintage equipment. We had figured out how to permanently locate an overhead projector on a cart and a TV/VCR on a tall cart in every classroom. By emptying out all of the classroom equipment in each department's own storage room, we found enough equipment for every classroom, so instructors did not have to lug one or two carts to their classrooms. Still, many faculty members wanted to use the Internet in classes and we had only one computer projection cart for the whole college.

The key to converting to a high-technology classroom was a ceiling projection system through which computer or other signals would be projected on a wall and a wired instructor station combined with a desk from which the instructor could make technology happen. We connected the ceiling projector not only to computer wires but also to a VCR and to a unit new to us, a video projection machine that looked somewhat like an overhead projector and took its place. This video projection machine, nicknamed "elmo," provides a much greater range of projection possibilities by underlighting, overlighting, and zooming. In addition to showing acetate pages, it can project an open book, a textile sample, a rock specimen, or even the class itself.

When we used our scarce college funds, we did not actually park a computer in the room, we just installed the wiring so that a faculty laptop computer could easily be hooked up. When we had state funding for the room, we bought a desktop computer for it, postponing the haunting worry about how we would pay for its inevitable replacement.

We enlarged the picture from the ceiling projector by having our maintenance staff apply thin-coat plaster to a large wall area, making a permanent screen on the wall. This was not only inexpensive but allowed us to avoid the usual problems with pull-down screens.

We designed a simple wired instructor station that our maintenance staff built for us at a fraction of the price of commercial furniture. For rooms with computers installed, we sank the monitor below the table level so that the entire table surface was usable.

Adding technology to classes not only enabled classes to go live but also allowed us to remove the overhead projectors and TV/VCRs on the tall stands, thereby creating more space.

Impact

Faculty and staff in the college have expanded their repertoire of classroom activities in our new rooms. One often observes small groups at work, student-led poster sessions at various boards, or students using the technology to make presentations. Tables provide natural groupings for discussion or other class work. Several tables put together provide for a larger discussion group. While the old tablet chair reinforced the individuality of the person sitting in it, carefully tucked in and separated from others by the tablet, the common tables reinforce the collective nature of the small group.

Changes in classrooms are visual and startling, giving faculty and staff in the college a heightened sense of empowerment, since they identified this need and can daily see the results of their resolve. They report that students also enjoy the changes and feel that teaching must be valued in our college. Said one student: "It looks like someone cares about our learning environment." Indeed, more than any other action we took to focus on teaching and learning, the classroom upgrades trumpeted our new goal. We surveyed faculty in our fourth year of renovations to ask their reactions to the new spaces; 90 percent of the replies urged us to continue. A sample reaction: "[The renovated classrooms] inspire instructors to create active learning opportunities for their students and allow them to integrate technology as a model of instruction." From another faculty member: "I have a sense now that at least in our college, the administration puts teaching and learning at the highest priority, which affirms my work." And another: "I believe that the use of new technology tried out in various classes has resulted in better dissemination of content information." And finally: "My students have become more willing to ask and answer questions in class. They now appear to be more interested in the process of learning and problem solving than just 'what the right answer is.'"

Lessons Learned

I think it is a Chinese proverb that says to be careful about what you ask for, because you might get it. The issue of unintended consequences looms large after major changes in classrooms.

"Don't touch that chair!" One problem we created stemmed from our universally endorsed, joyous move to flexible furniture. Why were we surprised when classes actually moved the furniture? The interior architecture students and I exhausted all scientifically possible ways to arrange the furniture, often taking into account over thirty arrangements during countless

hours of research. So when the furniture arrived, we arranged it in our prize-winning design. No wonder I began to develop body tics when I passed by classrooms arranged in different configurations, often with unused tables haphazardly stacked on top of each other. And then the complaints started from instructors whose idea of ideal space clashed with the previous instructors' ideas. The lecturers and the "discussants" could come to fisticuffs over this physical embodiment of their differences. How does one solve this chicken-and-egg dilemma? Should the students lose the first or the last five minutes of their classes moving furniture? And with all this moving, and stacking, and moving, how is the furniture itself holding up? I began to long for the days of simple tablet chairs that seemed to stay put or were so easily moved that no one complained.

"Give us some elbow room." Another troublesome consequence we are still dodging is that one can put more tablet chairs into a space than chairs at tables. Giving students needed table space takes up more room than stuffing them into those skinny little tablet chairs. We were all so happy that students would have better-quality space that we skimmed over the quantity issue. I think we were so dazzled with the innovations that we just assumed that there would be enough smaller classes to use the new rooms. But we did not consider where exactly the classes with the larger enrollments would go. Where they went is to the dean's office to complain! Now, several years later, students in classes of twenty-eight scheduled in rooms that hold twenty-four like the table arrangements enough to endure how close the tables and chairs are to each other. And we have worked to better match class size to class location, as well as expand some rooms.

"It's not the investment, it's the upkeep." While we wanted the classrooms to look and feel like a nice conference center, we had not taken into account the implications for maintenance and cleaning. The old plastic barrel chairs with their plastic tablets needed little upkeep or cleaning, and linoleum floors did fine with occasional sweeping and a yearly wax job. The new upholstered chairs and light laminate tops shouted for attention by the end of the first year, and the carpet stains sat too long for easy wiping up. While the maintenance staff was initially supportive of our changes, they probably focused too much on our agreement that the carpets did not have to be vacuumed every night like the linoleum had. We still have not conquered this hill either, but we have added new cleaning routines at the end of every semester.

"We've got the white board blues." Faculty and students expressed glee and jubilation when the white boards were installed—and then gloom and desolation several days later when the boards no longer erased. Who could have known that less expensive white boards were not intended for heavy classroom use, even two days of classroom use? Luckily, we were able to replace the first round of white boards with a second round that was more suitable and continues to erase years later. This year we plan to experiment with a new product, a dry erasable wall covering that can be wallpapered over blackboards or white boards that have hit the end of their useful life.

The white boards also presented other new challenges. We never had much of a problem with people walking off with chalk, but dry erasable markers had an initial shelf life of barely two days. Although the fad has run its course by now, we certainly underestimated the initial replacements required. This problem was exacerbated because the maintenance staff no longer kept the supply of blackboard chalk flowing, since they thought everyone was using the white boards. For a while instructors were carrying their own personal markers to class.

Cleaning white boards is also more complex than the swiping the simple dust eraser across a blackboard. There are several kinds of hard erasers, tear-off sheets, and liquid sprays, plus the worry that red or green little flakes will stain clothing.

"Don't write on that desk!" The design professionals reminded me that the greater contrast between a surface's color and papers used on the tables, the greater the eye strain. So in our first set of rooms, we created a calming, tone-on-tone light beige theme for tables, chairs, and flooring. Thereafter, I created another rule: the lighter the surface, the more it craves an artist's touch. The light-colored chairs, carpets, and floorboards also spotlighted stains, scuffs, and accidents, so our more recent classrooms sport more defensive darker colors.

While most people fancy themselves as capable of picking out colors for classrooms as they are for their own clothes, the urge should be stifled. If one person makes the choice, many people have to live with that person's personal preferences—and that person has to take the daily guff from those with different tastes! We found that using students and faculty in interior architecture or art and also getting additional opinions before making color choices helped us survive the gauntlet of opinions.

"Overhead smashes elmo?" The video-projection device or "elmo" was a shoo-in to replace the overhead projector, we thought. It projects a greater variety of things, eliminates making overheads, zooms in and out, and the camera can scan the classroom itself. Traditionalists counter that the overhead projector shows vertical images like most of their own notes, while the elmo's projection screen favors horizontal. They note that the old workhorse's images are sharper at a distance than the elmo's. Camps are forming; we recently had an e-mail debate over removing overhead projectors from rooms that already have elmos.

Conclusions

We made a lot of mistakes, corrected them on the next round, and discovered new mistakes. But we kept going, knowing that with each new space, flawed this way or that, we were creating our own new reality, a reality that keeps shouting, "Teaching counts!" Both students and faculty are urging the college to continue to focus on teaching in general and on learning spaces in particular. As we look ahead at new materials, new spaces, and new challenges, new considerations emerge. How can we use hallway and outdoor spaces to facilitate learning? How might we use the new product, dry erasable wallpaper? Is it possible to use the psychology of color for better learning environments? What physical changes might facilitate small learning communities in large classrooms?

The sheer magnitude of the inventory of older classrooms across the country shouting for passage into the twenty-first century is staggering. Yet we have found that overcoming the tendency to become overwhelmed and instead forging ahead room by room can be exciting and successful. I suppose we can endorse the observation of the old newspaper cartoon character, Pogo, who said: "We face almost insurmountable opportunities."

JOAN DEGUIRE NORTH is dean of the College of Professional Studies at University of Wisconsin–Stevens Point.

9

Several exciting spaces at colleges and universities throughout the country show how the built environment can enhance learning.

Innovative Models of Learning Environments

William Dittoe

Designers of educational spaces have always instinctively known that the built environment has a profound effect on its occupants. Yet little research has been available regarding this gut feeling. With the vast improvements in our understanding of teaching and learning that have occurred in the past decade, it is now quite clear that the classroom is much more than a neutral setting—it is a place that must by its very essence support and encourage learning. Unfortunately, most of the typical classrooms found across the land are totally inadequate for this important function. The traditional response to the design of learning environments—line up rooms and fill them with static tablet chairs—has greatly inhibited many creative educators by its inflexibility. At the same time there has been little challenge to architects to follow advances in pedagogy and understand why their designs perpetuate what Barr and Tagg (1995) have termed the "instructional paradigm" and hinder the move to active learning.

This chapter will describe spaces that are responsive to the learning paradigm, with the nuances of function, flexibility, and aesthetics necessary to bring the built environment and the educational environment into a harmonious learning relationship. This is a challenge, for this relationship involves not only size and shape and bricks and mortar but also light and color and the essential ambiance that stimulates emotional connections and allows the engagement and inquisitiveness necessary for deep learning. This task is also formidable because so very little has yet been tried, assessed, and understood regarding what architectural response best fits the learning paradigm.

The focus of this chapter will be to show, through built projects, examples that represent the ideas found in earlier chapters. These examples will

NEW DIRECTIONS FOR TEACHING AND LEARNING, no. 92, Winter 2002   © Wiley Periodicals, Inc.

highlight different design responses to certain educational needs, outlining how they came about, defining their goals, detailing design concepts, and providing some assessment as to how they are functioning.

Educators who read this chapter are likely thinking about learning spaces from an educational point of view; considering them as places for creating intellectual stimulation to provide opportunities for learning. For an architect, a learning environment is a place in time and space—a physical reality. It is the bricks and mortar that are used to form the learning environment. It is important to join these two viewpoints in the creation of educational spaces. Enormous power and creativity can occur when architects are exposed to new ways of thinking about teaching and learning. For example, some years ago, the architects in one of the firms involved in these examples were paired with an educator who talked with them about new approaches to teaching and learning and shared some of the key literature on these developments with them. That exchange led to productive new ways of envisioning learning spaces, concretely expressed in the environments that were built. Similar enhancement occurs when educators learn about the architectural viewpoint and about new developments in space design.

The following are examples of projects that are exciting in their design concepts and sometimes surprisingly simple in providing uncomplicated spaces to allow creative and spontaneous learning. They are different from each other because they have different goals. They are similar as well in that they are earnest efforts to provide responsive built environments that encourage students to take charge, with proper guidance, of their own education.

The projects will be considered in terms of how they affect the behavior of their occupants—whether they achieve the quest for environments that are student-centered and empowering. The descriptions will also focus on how the projects have affected the educational process in terms of space, furnishings, and equipment, the capacity to be functional and flexible, and provision of appropriate atmosphere and technology sufficient for the educational purpose. Functionality deals with the ability of the spaces to accommodate the educational purpose, while flexibility is the ability to easily and quickly adapt to myriad functions. Atmosphere is the use of shapes, color, and lighting along with purposeful attempts at personalization to fashion an environment that promotes and encourages freedom, collaboration, and creativity.

The Math Emporium, Virginia Tech

The Math Emporium was conceived, planned, and executed with little help from architects. A true grassroots effort, it found its beginning in the early 1990s as it became desirable to introduce information technology into math programs. The increased use of technology, larger student enrollments, and the state legislature's funding of pilot programs compelled the university to set up the Math Emporium in a vacant department store close to the main campus. The facility is large, open, and inviting, with high ceilings remaining from its retail past. One enters the spacious building to see a reception desk to the left with a small, inviting lounge opposite furnished with comfortable tables, chairs, and couches. The main focus of attention, however, is the vista seen straight ahead and wrapping behind the reception area for a considerable distance. An eye-catching five hundred computers in pods of six fill this space, which is usually a hive of activity. The twenty-four-hour facility is not a computer center but a true learning community that focuses on math. Tucked in the far corners are an open classroom and conference space partly hidden by head-high screens. Offices and workrooms are available and accessed from a small faculty lounge. All functions except the offices are within the large high space.

Most of the work being done in the Math Emporium is self-paced. Faculty members, with the assistance of selected students, are on a rotating schedule and available for assistance from early morning to late into the evening. Students may work alone or in groups and have access to numerous tutorial programs and Web-based lectures. Conversation may continue in the comfortable lounge or scheduled lectures may occur in the corner classroom or elsewhere in the facility.

So how well does the Math Emporium work when you consider that little professional space planning was involved? Actually quite well. The main charm comes from the fact that there is nothing pretentious about it. No grand design statement or deep allegorical meanings here. It is just a large space and it honestly remains so. The space stays relatively quiet even with the large number of people doing various tasks. Attempts have been made to brighten it up by wrapping support columns with different patterns, but in reality the people and computers give it its character, color, and life. Some professional design assistance might have introduced subtler accent lighting and separated the different functions better. Still, the Math Emporium works and serves its purpose effectively. One of the main deficiencies comes from the circular computer pods. Collaboration is limited to discussion with people directly adjacent or standing behind the user as the shape and height of the computers prohibits anything more. Perhaps in the future, laptops, wireless connections, and movable furniture can improve collaborative group meetings while maintaining the original concept.

The Math Emporium sees most of the university's students, especially in the first two years, come through its doors. The best statistics, however, are the positive impact on learning efficiency, improved student-faculty communications, higher grades, and improved retention and failure rates that Virginia Tech has been able to report. The Math Emporium is also forging new collaborations with other disciplines such as economics, biology, and business. The charm of this successful endeavor lies in its simplicity. A need to improve learning was perceived, a space to house it was found, and the project was, by hard work and persistence, achieved.

The Prototype Laptop Classroom, Ohio Dominican College

When Ohio Dominican College in Columbus, Ohio, committed to becoming a laptop computer institution it seemed logical to make serious investigations into what types of learning environments would be required. The college was encouraging its students to take full advantage of the computer, and soon the familiar black toting case became a campus fixture. Ohio Dominican had pursued student-centered, project-oriented, and technology-intense learning since the inception of its Invitation to Tomorrow project, a faculty-initiated review of curriculum in 1994. However, it quickly became obvious that traditional classrooms did not support new concepts in teaching and learning.

Since 1994 the college has invested countless hours and significant funds to create learning environments that provide efficient and flexible space responsive to diverse pedagogies. Among the first innovations was the semicircular computer classroom featuring round tables for collaboration. Computer "labs" were set up in clusters in public environments.

The most recent foray is the planning of a prototype laptop classroom that will test applications of spatial arrangements, lighting, flexible furnishings, and technology. This nontraditional space began by engaging architects to study just how a typical classroom of about six hundred square feet could be converted to a new learning environment. The result was the laptop classroom prototype.

The design objective was to create an experimental space that would accept courses from the normally scheduled curriculum. This space was to be fitted with technology appropriate for the laptop connections, audiovisual support, and flexibility of furnishings for arrangement into multiple configurations. Improvement over typical sterile classroom environments was also a primary design issue.

During the planning process, the architects facilitated meetings with the professors who would initially use the new room. Faculty from English, mathematics, and other core subjects would be testing models for the new space. Assessment to understand how the space functioned, what pedagogical methods were successful, and what elements in teaching and learning were ineffective was important to the final outcome. The college chose a standard classroom on the second floor of a mixed-use building in the heart of campus. One enters the space from a double-loaded corridor near offices and other classrooms. The first impression on entering is of walking into a quiet living room or perhaps an upscale corporate boardroom. It is subtler in lighting and richer in color than typical classrooms. The rows of standard desks have been replaced with softly sculpted tables and large padded armchairs. Portraits reflecting the college's Dominican heritage hang on the walls, and the west-facing windows are shaded to carefully filter the light while still allowing intriguing views of the foliage beyond. Even the white boards lining two walls have an appearance that indicates that what is put upon them is valued and important. To the rear, in a recessed alcove, is the technology grouping that allows control of the computers, audiovisual equipment, and other systems used daily.

A slight ramp at the entry conceals the two-inch false floor that gives access to the electric and data wiring beneath a floral-patterned carpet. Carpet squares were selected to add richness to the environment while also providing simple access and sound control. Above, the high white ceiling is accented with an open two-foot by two-foot metal grid painted soft lavender and positioned to float as an element of sculptural interest. The lighting is simple in concept. Six white dishes provide up-lighting that reflects from the ceiling, bringing soft nonglare illumination necessary for computer work and visual projections. Spots from adjustable light tracks highlight the walls and white boards. The combination, simply controlled and dimmable, provides adequate lighting for most academic tasks. Computers are wired from the raised floor into demountable pedestals placed about the room; the movable tables are clustered around these ports with students working independently or in groups of four to six.

A typical class in English composition will see students enter the room, some early, to be greeted by sounds of a Chopin sonata and the sight of the course Web page projected on the wall screen. Students come prepared by previously reviewing the day's class expectations by the way of their computers. The session begins as the professor reviews main issues for a short time. Most of the remaining class is spent in group activities, student presentations, or quiet individual work. With all the activity, the room remains remarkably peaceful and respect for one another is evident. One also observes that the common barrier between teacher and student has been deemphasized and that while there is a relaxed mood, sometimes punctuated with soft laughter, the overall atmosphere remains serious and productive. Student comments are extremely positive and indicate an awareness of the room's aesthetics and affirmation of how it plays an important role in learning. Assistance during class time comes not only from the professor but also from active involvement and sharing between students.

Evaluations of the space and learning are currently being conducted. To date the assessments have been positive. Some issues such as glare on the white boards from the spotlights and limited flexibility due to the wiring pedestals have to be considered and refined. Understanding the effects of the space on learning will take time as assessment methods need to be established and evaluated over a longer period. All in all, most are pleased with the first prototype and plans for extending the model in other areas of the college are under way.

The Studio, University of Dayton

The Learning-Teaching Center was planned to become the heart and soul of the campus community. Its purpose is to become a place of challenge, providing an atmosphere of collaboration, conversation, experimentation, and reflection. Major spaces within the center include offices for faculty development, the learning village, and service learning, as well as a learning assistance center and media support. There are also groupware and seminar areas, specialized testing, and research space all arranged around a central rotunda that functions as hub and main gathering space. Other key areas such as the café and an intimate fireplace lounge were incorporated to encourage socializing, provide opportunities for creative discourse, and promote relaxation. The LTC even has an experimental classroom that allows faculty and students to explore and develop better teaching and learning strategies. This space, called the Studio, has been in operation for two semesters and the initial evaluations indicate a major positive impact upon learning.

The Studio is accessed from a short corridor off the main pathway through the LTC. It is directly across from the Forum, a multifunction space designed primarily to house seminars, meetings, and small conferences. These two spaces are designed to complement each other and be used in tandem to support larger functions with multiple uses. A few paces away from this educational complex finds the Blend, a student-operated café, and various seating configurations that offer impromptu opportunities for continued classroom discussions or quiet personal reflection.

The Studio itself is a thirty-foot by thirty-foot space with a white ceiling at about ten feet. A modified metal grid, painted light tan, is suspended from above at eight feet from the floor and divides the room into thirds forming nine quadrants. Two walls contain a mounting system that allows two-foot by three-foot demountable white boards to be used individually, grouped into a long series or moved to the overhead beams that make up the suspended grid. The off-white walls are striped with a subtle dark horizontal line at two-foot intervals to provide visual reference points while adding interest to the space. The floor is covered with a patterned carpet in dark purple tones.

Adjustable lighting is achieved by the hanging strip fixtures that allow indirect or direct light, or a combination of the two. Supplemental lighting is provided by dimmable down-lights mounted near the walls. The Studio is not intended to be a showpiece of technology but to have technology accessible and adequate for the university's typical curriculum. Wireless computer connections are available as well as numerous wall ports for power and data. The room is connected to the sophisticated campus data system and accessed as needed for various class requirements including smart board use. One of the Studio's walls is devoted to storage of audiovisual equipment, coats and bags, extra chairs, and other "let's get it out of the way" issues. The furnishings were carefully selected to provide comfort, durability, and especially flexibility by being easily movable. Investigations into furniture designed for corporate settings showed that this type of furniture was far preferable to that normally available for higher education. Chapter Four tells this interesting tale.

How does one evaluate learning occurring within the Studio? This important question is being pondered as those who have facilitated courses are gathering to discuss just how they are using the space and how it is affecting learning. Telling testimony was provided by the reaction of a student upon entering the Learning-Teaching Center for the first time. "Wow, this is a seriously cool place!" While this reaction is important and shows that people can indeed be aware of and impressed by the built environment, the question remains—and is being asked—are people learning more, and better? The assessment process is far from complete. In fact, the proper questions to ask are just being formulated. Therefore, perhaps the best way to relate how the space is being used is to share the most recent comments from debriefing meetings.

First of all the university determined that those who wished to facilitate classes in the Studio would submit a paper as to why and how they would use the space, and proposals would be selected from that group. Various classes such as math, philosophy, chemical engineering, religion, and others have taken place. Since then, many of the involved faculty have meet to discuss the space, educational methods used, and reactions and observations of both professors and students. It is interesting to note that one of the more common experiences shared was that the space allowed both professor and student to be "different." The teacher-student relationships became freer and more equitable than the traditional model. A few comments support this finding: "I feel and act differently. There is no head of the room." "This space says 'Let's learn together.'" "The room lets people loosen up." A genuine freedom has been imparted to the students; they have been empowered and are now, in positive ways, taking more responsibility for their learning. One professor describes a course taught in a standard campus classroom as being in typical teacher-as-pontificator style with passive students. When another session of the same course met in the Studio, however, the professor said the students would get up, take the marker, and make their point on the white boards without being requested to do so. This development was seen in very positive terms by the faculty. Further evaluation is necessary to determine just why these results are occurring, but obviously something extremely positive is happening in this new environment.

Another very important issue occurring at Dayton's Learning-Teaching Center involves connections. As one facilitator put it, "I can walk out of the Studio and continue important discussions. I'm not in just a hall but in the café or the fireplace lounge." In other words, the entire complex is a learning environment and supports the learning process from space to space. Observations, assessment, and sharing of lessons learned will continue. Something educationally stimulating and of great value is obviously occurring. It will take some time to figure out just what and why. But it is working.

Isom Academic Center, Ohio Valley College

Ohio Valley College, a small Christian liberal arts college nestled within the hills of Parkersburg, West Virginia, is experiencing remarkable growth. When the college had the opportunity to purchase a 1960s-vintage seminary adjacent to the campus, its future brightened, but new important issues arose. Could facilities originally designed for high school students easily become an environment supportive of the college's mission? How best could the secluded hilltop setting become a vibrant, student-centered campus?

A long-range campus development plan that clearly defined space needs was created to focus on becoming a student-centered campus. The plan calls for numerous hybrid spaces to provide a continuous flow of educational and community-enriching experiences.

The building purchased contained a three-story wing that became known as the Isom Academic Center. A concept plan was developed to allow the existing classrooms to be reconfigured to provide more flexible and varied educational programs. The ground floor, previously containing four oversized classrooms and a large multi-use student lounge, was redesigned by converting two of the classrooms into three smaller (twenty-four to twenty-six student) flexible learning environments. The other two rooms directly across the hall were removed to create an open space overlooking a future garden. This area will provide a large breakout and study area designed to allow group activities adjacent to the learning environments. A small café will allow students and faculty to gather in a serious but more relaxed atmosphere. The remaining area will become a tiered case-study space that is flexible enough to accommodate up to a hundred participants.

The first floor was redesigned to be the initial prototype learning environment. This will include a classroom with adjacent seminar rooms that will test flexible table and chair arrangements, lighting, and audiovisual components. The atmosphere will also be improved with new colors and shapes that will immediately change the existing bland environment. An adjoining space, a sixty-foot by sixty-foot open room used for various functions, will become a learning center providing faculty and students a place to test better ways of teaching and learning. The second floor will be reconfigured into hybrid laboratory space. The college is still considering what assessment methods will be the most effective to track the educational merits of the design.

Innovative Classrooms at Rensselaer Polytechnic Institute

Dating from the 1980s, experiments with the ways in which physics instruction was delivered at Rensselaer, in Troy, N.Y., led to the need for new kinds of facilities to support classroom activity, not only in physics but also across other disciplines that had adopted new approaches to course design based on the experiments. The result was the studio classroom.

Studio classrooms at Rensselaer vary from room to room, with two predominant designs—the cluster configuration and the theater-in-the-round configuration. Cluster classrooms situate two to four students at tables around a single workstation. The clusters are arranged in rooms that have normal projection space along one wall but are otherwise flexible with respect to where the instructor is stationed. Often, there is display space all around the room so that students can work at white boards or chalkboards with their peers or the instructor. In these spaces, the instructor can circulate easily while students work, or can stand at one location easily seen and heard by students, who can swing their chairs around to obtain a good sight line.

In the theater-in-the-round configuration, students work two at a table supporting either one or two computers. The tables are arranged in concentric ovals, often in tiers, with the instructor station at one end and the student chairs on the inside of each oval. Students turn their chairs to the center for whole group discussion or lecture and away from the center for work on the computers. This arrangement prevents students from being distracted by the workstations while they are interacting or listening and affords the instructor a view of the screens from the center when the students are using the computers. An example of the studio at Rensselaer can be accessed through the Web site for this volume at http://spacesfor learning.udayton.edu.

Similar facilities are available in many institutions, often in business and law school environments as well as in science and engineering classes. While the aesthetics and acoustics may vary enormously, the basic design permits teachers to move fluidly from whole-group to small-group activity, from presentation to active engagement. These arrangements have recently been aided by the introduction of wireless environments and laptop computers, which alleviate the usual encumbrances of wiring and limited work space.

Rensselaer is also the home of the RPI Collaborative Classroom, designed to support work in which students must approach projects from a team perspective. At first, classrooms equipped to promote collaboration grouped seating around one stationary computer or used laptops. The need for common display space and the availability of integrated keyboards and mice led to a new design configuration using "tulip-shaped" tables that permit two to six students to be seated at a table, preserving sight lines to each other as well as to the instructor's console. Supported by special software and servers, student laptops are used to share control of the public machine located at the table. The arrangement allows instructor demonstration, peer learning, team meetings, instructor consultation, client consultation, and presentation and critique. Design specifications can be accessed through the Web site for this volume at http://spacesforlearning.udayton.edu.

Summary

Many other attempts to enrich the learning environment are under way, some grassroots efforts, some incorporating design professionals. The associated Web page for this volume (http://spacesforlearning.udayton.edu)

displays photos and diagrams of some of these environments. These spaces reveal the subtle yet profound ways in which surroundings affect activity. It is disturbing to accept the bland classrooms of today as suitable for the most important of human endeavors—learning. The spaces described in this chapter, as well as other innovative spaces at campuses across the country, are testimony to the power of design to promote deep learning.

Reference

Barr, R. B., and Tagg, J. "From Teaching to Learning: A New Paradigm for Undergraduate Education." *Change,* Nov./Dec. 1995, 27(4), 13–25.

WILLIAM DITTOE *is an architect with extensive experience working with colleges and universities. He is a principal of Educational Facilities Consultants, LLC, a firm that specializes in the design of the built environment for higher education.*

10

The need for change in the design of learning spaces demands radical rethinking of many powerful traditional assumptions, yet this activity is vital to the success of higher education in the future.

Improving the Environment for Learning: An Expanded Agenda

Nancy Van Note Chism, Deborah J. Bickford

The decade of the 1990s was a powerful period for focusing attention on learning. Ernest Boyer's (1990) *Scholarship Reconsidered* ushered in the decade, helping to broaden the conception of what should be valued by the Academy. Barr and Tagg's (1995) oft-cited piece "From Teaching to Learning" put into words what many had been experiencing, the sometimes painful move toward focusing on student learning—the outcome of teaching efforts, rather than the efforts themselves. Donald (1997), in *Improving the Environment for Learning: Academic Leaders Talk About What Works,* reported the results of interviews of academic leaders in four universities, focusing not on the usual topics such as resources or research productivity but on discerning what these leaders felt could be done to improve the learning environment. Yet throughout this discussion, not one of the issues raised had to do with the physical environment in which learning takes place. Hopefully, the perspectives offered in this *New Directions in Teaching and Learning* volume demonstrate clearly that physical space does make a difference.

As the messages regarding learning are translated into change, there is a need to recognize, however belatedly, that new visions must be characterized by differences in the way that higher education institutions think about, plan, allocate resources for, and use learning spaces. The need for change is supported by the arguments made by the authors within this volume.

First are the implications of research on how learning occurs. The need for active engagement, social interaction, and physical comfort in learning situations is well supported by the evidence from researchers in many disciplines. Findings from environmental psychology support the emphasis on improved learning spaces, based on principles dealing with comfort, aesthetics, information display and control, and communication as influenced by environmental attitudes and place attachment, lighting and temperature, and density and noise.

In addition, the inspirational value of good learning spaces is affirmed by Vaughan (1991): "Good rooms enable good teaching. A rich network of interstitial spaces both inside and out ensures that the joy of teaching and learning extends beyond the classroom. . . . Curricula can inspire good architecture, but good architecture can also inspire a new understanding of teaching and learning" (p. 12).

These arguments are buttressed by additional market considerations. Faced with competition from virtual universities, corporate learning divisions, and other routes to education now available to potential students, traditional colleges and universities cannot afford to underestimate the importance of place as an element of competitive advantage. The memories that alumni have are acutely connected to physical aspects of their alma maters. Institutional development offices understand this attachment in raising funds. Prospective students and the parents of traditional-age students have elevated expectations for comfort, aesthetics, modern technology, and convenience in judging both residential and learning spaces. Consequently, colleges and universities that neglect the potential advantage of physical space through failing to devote adequate resources or engaging in poor planning routinely present a less compelling case for both fundraising and recruitment.

In addition to the marketing aspects, learning spaces have an important symbolic value for those within the academic community. Creating spaces thoughtfully and with the involvement of users, providing adequate resources for aesthetics, comfort, and functionality, and maintaining them to high standards are actions that say that an institution cares about teaching and learning and regards them as central activities to its mission. As Fenton (1991) pointed out in his analysis of the effects of classroom renovations at Carnegie Mellon University, "Improved classrooms have sent a quiet message to faculty members: the University cares about quality teaching and will make substantial efforts to provide the facilities that can improve both teaching and learning" (p. 247). An institution that proclaims a value on teaching and learning in its mission yet situates faculty and students in inadequate spaces is displaying its conflicted messages quite openly each day. An institution that proclaims learner-centered instruction yet builds rooms that focus on the teacher and ignore the need for learner comfort and interaction is similarly contradicting itself.

The Road to Improvement

Institutions intent on improving their learning spaces can find direction through the advice and examples on the planning process and design alternatives offered throughout this volume. In addition, several others have summarized characteristics of ideal learning spaces. For example, Blackett and Stanfield (1994) offer the following basic list: plan for the full range of teaching modalities, plan for change and flexibility, and focus on the exchange of ideas and the acquisition of knowledge. To these, Jilk (1998) adds the following:

- Strong identification with the institution
- Integration within the wider community to take advantage of community-based resources
- Flexibility or adaptability
- Interaction support (creating a sense of smallness to foster work on common goals)
- Access to technology
- Support for research and service, as well as for teaching

Niemeyer's (n.d.) list of design principles focuses on practices that empower faculty, emphasize flexibility, encourage interaction, stress simplicity, expand connectivity, contain costs, and "sweat details." Among his specific recommendations are such tips as "Faculty prefer wide but not deep classrooms," "You can't provide too much chalkboard," "Switch lights parallel to the front of the room," and "Create curved rows and no teacher's platform."

Across the sets of principles in this volume and in the literature, the stress is on flexibility (a factor in every list), support for interaction, ease of technology use, and match to learning goals.

So What's Stopping Us?

In addition to resources, one of the chief factors preventing the creation of good learning spaces is the body of persistent, often tacit, assumptions that hamper our thinking and action. These are listed in Table 10.1.

Replacing assumptions that have barely been consciously articulated with new foundational ideas will not be easy, yet often the very act of surfacing assumptions for thoughtful consideration and debate is a powerful starting point.

Designing Learning Spaces with Learning as a Primary Purpose: A New Action Agenda

Boyatzis, Cowen, and Kolb (1995), in *Innovation in Professional Education,* pose a provocative question: What if learning were the purpose of education? They acknowledge that all might agree that learning is a purpose of education—"but is it the primary purpose?" (p. 229). Building on their thoughts, the remainder of this chapter responds to the question of how spaces (real and virtual) would be designed if learning were the primary purpose of education.

Table 10.1. From the Old to the New in Learning Space Design

Old Assumption	New Assumption	Implications
Learning only happens in classrooms.	Learning happens everywhere.	The whole campus is potentially a learning space. Corridors, lobbies, outdoor spaces can all be arranged to promote learning.
Learning happens at fixed times.	Learning happens any time.	It is important to invest in scheduling systems that make learning spaces available on a flexible basis.
Learning is an individual activity.	Learning is very much influenced by the social environment.	A prime consideration in learning space design must be the facilitation of social interaction.
What happens in classrooms is pretty much the same from class to class and day to day.	Differences in course goals and teaching methods from day to day and course to course require different spaces.	A variety of classroom spaces need to be available. Flexibility to rearrange spatial configurations within a room is also important.
A classroom always has a front.	Classroom configuration depends on activity.	Classrooms rigidly oriented with the presumption that presentation will be the only mode of instruction will not accommodate other approaches.
Learning demands privacy and removal of distractions.	Learning is aided by openness and stimuli.	Learning spaces should flow into adjoining areas rather than be closed off and should contain interesting objects and decor.
Windows distract students from learning.	Windows provide needed light and sense of openness.	Windows should not be sacrificed to create closed spaces. Darkening for technology should be accomplished by shades or other devices rather than by building rooms without windows.
Flexibility can be enhanced by filling rooms with as many chairs as will fit.	Rooms crowded with furniture may ease the job of those who schedule them but not those who learn in them.	Standard per-student space allocation within a room should be expanded over current norms. Stackable and movable furniture should be chosen when possible to create more floor space when there are fewer learners.
Higher education students are juvenile. They will destroy or steal expensive furnishings. They need to be confined to tablet arm chairs to feel like students. They are all young, small, nimble, and without disabilities.	Students are adults. When put in an environment with dignified surroundings and furnishings, they will act appropriately. They require furnishings that accommodate physical differences.	Learning environment spaces in academia must resemble corporate environments rather than elementary schools. Furnishings and room decor need to be dignified and comfortable.
Amplification in large rooms is only necessary to hear the instructor or technology.	Even in large rooms, students as well as faculty need to be heard. Students can and should learn from each other.	Amplification and acoustics are important whole-room considerations in lecture halls or other large learning spaces.
Furniture needs to be purchased only when new spaces are created.	There is an ongoing need for furniture replacement and upgrade.	Continuing budget allocations for learning space furnishings need to be available, both for new purchases and replacement.
Architects. . . Facilities managers. . . Campus administrators. . . Faculty. . . Students. . . . . . know best when it comes to planning learning spaces.	The planning of learning spaces requires true collaboration among the multiple actors involved.	The design process should be conceived to permit broad participation, with priorities on learning considerations.

If learning really mattered, would faculty choose to teach classes in the learning spaces that all-too-frequently constitute the teaching infrastructures at today's colleges and universities? The answer is obvious. Why the need for change? Is it because learning really doesn't matter, or because there is not enough understanding of the crucial role that space plays in shaping learning environments? One of the purposes of this volume has been to highlight the latter point—that space *does* make a difference. Armed with this understanding, what are the next steps?

What would happen differently if institutions were to recognize the effect of learning space on learning? First, they would devote significant resources to understand better how learning does take place and the role of physical space in the learning process. Faculty, staff, and administrators would study university systems and processes from different perspectives, instead of devoting the lion's share of academic attention to critiquing and understanding other institutions' work environments, systems, and processes. In other words, institutions would be more adept at focusing critical thinking on their own environments instead of passing over them. They would recognize and value the important work that needs to be conducted in understanding not only the content of academic disciplines but also the effective, indeed the superlative, ways of helping people *learn* these disciplines. They would value research from all disciplines that would address learning issues—not confine such inquiry primarily to the education and educational psychology disciplines. They would create spaces on campuses to foster experimentation and reflection and learning by students and faculty, and encourage and value research output resulting from such efforts.

What is needed to stimulate this kind of intellectual curiosity about and progress in developing excellent learning environments? Six major actions can help to move the agenda.

Increase Understanding of the Issues. Traditional structures, interests, and perspectives act relentlessly to erode innovation. To change understanding and policymaking about learning spaces meaningfully requires the involvement of the major players highlighted in Chapter Five. Legislators and donors, faculty, students, administrators, even architects and furniture makers need to be part of a dialogue aimed at gaining understanding and momentum around abandoning the old assumptions that guided decision making and supplanting them with a new understanding of how learning spaces shape learning. Given present realities, they need to consider what Ron Bleed (2001) calls "a hybrid campus for the new millennium," considering what functions will still require learning spaces on campus and what learning is best achieved virtually or in community settings. Faculty development centers can add this topic to their agenda, engaging faculty in dialogue about the influence of space on the learning of their students and advocating for change on their campuses.

Empower Decision Makers and Change Leaders. Diverse teams should be empowered to develop new spaces on campus (or renovate old ones), and provided with adequate funding (and even involvement in fund-raising), as well as good information. Learning to work on cross-functional teams takes time and patience. The work of such groups should be recognized as important and challenging, and rewarded.

Use Systems Thinking. Viewing learning as a process will be critical. The shaping and successful implementation of learning spaces involve not only facilities managers and architects but also faculty, students, and administrators. A systems view would also require input from instructional designers and course schedulers, to name just two. Interfaces with those who do room scheduling as well as those who build and renovate space are crucial. Each perspective is important, and designing for learning requires understanding the role each plays in the learning process.

Create Places to Experiment. Experimental learning spaces where standard teaching evaluations can be abandoned in favor of experimentation and communities of practice can be developed for faculty (and perhaps even students) to share their learnings. Such investments can help tremendously in reducing the erosion of innovation caused by traditional structures and mind-sets. New configurations, technology, and furniture combinations can be tried and the successful ideas transferred to other spots on campus, rather than having all the units reinvent the wheel by learning for themselves, thus creating both excitement and efficiencies.

Stimulate Action Research. There is so much we still don't know about the effects of physical space on the learning of specific disciplines. What are the barriers, institution by institution, to encouraging such action research? Stimulating action research may require anything from creating "safe zones" for experimentation to a review of promotion and tenure documents. A growing number of pedagogically oriented journals provide outlets for such scholarship; it's time to assess and remove barriers to the creation of such scholarship on the nation's campuses.

Develop Useful Assessment Methods. As faculty experiment with new learning spaces, they need assessment methods in place that will be able to capture the effects of change and allow units to learn from one another's experiments.

Summary

A remarkable confluence of ideas is converging on the issue of learning spaces. Through brain research we understand better now than ever before the value of active learning. External competition from corporate and for-profit universities is creating an awareness that change is needed. Cross-functional decision making, becoming more common in corporate settings, is being recognized on campuses as an important approach to facilitate change. A significant portion of our classrooms nationwide are in need of renovation or replacement. And a new paradigm favoring learning over teaching and active learning over passive knowledge absorption is making headway in changing our assumptions about how learning takes place, as well as creating the need for more research.

To take advantage of the opportunities that this confluence of ideas provides, it is necessary to acknowledge the importance of learning spaces, revise the ways in which institutions plan for them, and augment the role of faculty and student users in the decision making. Colleges and universities must abandon business-as-usual assumptions in constructing and renovating learning spaces to allow for consideration of the impact of such huge factors as technology, lifelong learning patterns, and demographics on the projected future use of these spaces. The present era demands radical rethinking rather than tinkering, and all are involved, from end users to furniture manufacturers, architects, and academic administrators. While the challenge is enormous, the work is creative and exciting, and most of all, fundamental to the quality of learning in the future. Higher education has no other option than to embrace it, should it intend to flourish in the coming years.

References

Barr, R. B., and Tagg, J. "From Teaching to Learning: A New Paradigm for Undergraduate Education." *Change,* Nov./Dec. 1995, 27(4), 13–25.

Blackett, A., and Stanfield, B. "A Planner's Guide to Tomorrow's Classrooms," *Planning for Higher Education,* Spring 1994, 22, 25–31.

Bleed, R. "A Hybrid Campus for the New Millennium." *Educause Review,* Jan.-Feb. 2001, 36, 16–24.

Boyatzis, R. E., Cowen, S. S., and Kolb, D. A. *Innovation in Professional Education.* San Francisco: Jossey-Bass, 1995.

Boyer, E. L. *Scholarship Reconsidered: Priorities of the Professoriate.* Princeton, N.J.: Carnegie Foundation for the Advancement of Teaching, 1990.

Donald, J. *Improving the Environment for Learning: Academic Leaders Talk About What Works.* San Francisco: Jossey-Bass, 1997.

Fenton, E. "Coping with the Academic 'Tragedy of the Commons': Renovating Classrooms at Carnegie Mellon University." In K. Zahorski (ed.), *To Improve the Academy,* no. 10. Stillwater, Okla.: New Forums Press, 1991.

Jilk, B. A. "Designing a Model for the College Campus of the Future," *AIArchitect,* Apr. 1998. [http://spacesforlearning.udayton.edu].

Niemeyer, D. "Classroom Design Principles That Improve Teaching and Learning," n.d. [http://spacesforlearning.udayton.edu].

Vaughan, T. "Good Teaching Rooms: A Campus Resource." *Academe,* July-Aug. 1991, 76(4), 11–15.

Nancy Van Note Chism is associate dean of the faculties and associate vice chancellor for professional development at Indiana University–Purdue University Indianapolis, and associate professor of higher education and student affairs at Indiana University.

Deborah J. Bickford is associate provost for learning, learning environments, and pedagogy, co-director of the Learning Village, and associate professor of management at the University of Dayton.

Index

Back Issue/Subscription Order Form

Copy or detach and send to:
Jossey-Bass, A Wiley Company, 989 Market Street, San Francisco CA 94103-1741

Call or fax toll-free: Phone 888-378-2537 6:30AM – 3PM PST; Fax 888-481-2665

Back Issues: Please send me the following issues at $27 each
(Important: please include ISBN number with your order.)

_____

_____

_____

$ _____ Total for single issues

$ _____ SHIPPING CHARGES: SURFACE   Domestic Canadian
First Item $5.00 $6.00
Each Add'l Item $3.00 $1.50
For next-day and second-day delivery rates, call the number listed above.

Subscriptions   Please ❑ start ❑ renew my subscription to *New Directions for Teaching and Learning* for the year 2___ at the following rate:

U.S.	❑ Individual $70	❑ Institutional $145
Canada	❑ Individual $70	❑ Institutional $185
All Others	❑ Individual $94	❑ Institutional $219
Online Subscription		❑ Institutional $145

**For more information about online subscriptions visit
www.interscience.wiley.com**

$ _____ Total single issues and subscriptions (Add appropriate sales tax for your state for single issue orders. No sales tax for U.S. subscriptions. Canadian residents, add GST for subscriptions and single issues.)

❑Payment enclosed (U.S. check or money order only)
❑VISA ❑ MC ❑ AmEx ❑ Discover Card #_____ Exp. Date _____

Signature _____ Day Phone _____
❑ Bill Me (U.S. institutional orders only. Purchase order required.)

Purchase order # _____
Federal Tax ID13559302   **GST 89102 8052**

Name _____

Address _____

_____

Phone _____ E-mail _____

For more information about Jossey-Bass, visit our Web site at www.josseybass.com

PROMOTION CODE ND03

focus groups, and creating questions that target individual faculty needs and interest.
ISBN: 0-7879-5789-5

TL86   **Scholarship Revisited: Perspectives on the Scholarship of Teaching**
Carolin Kreber
Presents the outcomes of a Delphi Study conducted by an international panel of academics working in faculty evaluation scholarship and postsecondary teaching and learning. Identifies the important components of scholarship of teaching, defines its characteristics and outcomes, and explores its most pressing issues.
ISBN: 0-7879-5447-0

TL85   **Beyond Teaching to Mentoring**
Alice G. Reinarz, Eric R. White
Offers guidelines to optimizing student learning through classroom activities as well as peer, faculty, and professional mentoring. Addresses mentoring techniques in technical training, undergraduate business, science, and liberal arts studies, health professions, international study, and interdisciplinary work.
ISBN: 0-7879-5617-1

TL84   **Principles of Effective Teaching in the Online Classroom**
Renée E. Weiss, Dave S. Knowlton, Bruce W. Speck
Discusses structuring the online course, utilizing resources from the World Wide Web and using other electronic tools and technology to enhance classroom efficiency. Addresses challenges unique to the online classroom community, including successful communication strategies, performance evaluation, academic integrity, and accessibility for disabled students.
ISBN: 0-7879-5615-5

TL83   **Evaluating Teaching in Higher Education: A Vision for the Future**
Katherine E. Ryan
Analyzes the strengths and weaknesses of current approaches to evaluating teaching and recommends practical strategies for improving current evaluation methods and developing new ones. Provides an overview of new techniques such as peer evaluations, portfolios, and student ratings of instructors and technologies.
ISBN: 0-7879-5448-9

TL82   **Teaching to Promote Intellectual and Personal Maturity: Incorporating Students' Worldviews and Identities into the Learning Process**
Marcia B. Baxter Magolda
Explores cognitive and emotional dimensions that influence how individuals learn, and describes teaching practices for building on these to help students develop intellectually and personally. Examines how students' unique understanding of their individual experience, themselves, and the ways knowledge is constructed can mediate learning.
ISBN: 0-7879-5446-2

TL81   **Strategies for Energizing Large Classes: From Small Groups to Learning Communities**
Jean MacGregor, James L. Cooper, Karl A. Smith, Pamela Robinson
Describes a comprehensive range of ideas and techniques from informal turn-to-your-neighbor discussions that punctuate a lecture to more complex

small-group activities, as well as ambitious curricular reform through learning-community structures.
ISBN: 0-7879-5337-7

TL80   **Teaching and Learning on the Edge of the Millennium: Building on What We Have Learned**
Marilla D. Svinicki
Reviews the past and current research on teaching, learning, and motivation. Chapters revisit the best-selling *NDTL* issues, exploring the latest developments in group-based learning, effective communication, teaching for critical thinking, the seven principles for good practice in undergraduate education, teaching for diversity, and teaching in the information age.
ISBN: 0-7879-4874-8

TL79   **Using Consultants to Improve Teaching**
Christopher Knapper, Sergio Piccinin
Provides advice on how to use consultation to improve teaching, giving detailed descriptions of a variety of effective approaches, including classroom observation, student focus groups, small-group instructional diagnosis, faculty learning communities, and action learning.
ISBN: 0-7879-4876-4

TL78   **Motivation from Within: Approaches for Encouraging Faculty and Students to Excel**
Michael Theall
Examines how students' cultural backgrounds and beliefs about knowledge affect their motivation to learn, and applies the latest motivational theory to the instructional process and the university community.
ISBN: 0-7879-4875-6

TL77   **Promoting Civility: A Teaching Challenge**
Steven M. Richardson
Offers strategies for promoting civil discourse and resolving conflict when it arises—both in the classroom and in the campus community at large. Recommends effective responses to disruptive classroom behavior and techniques for encouraging open, respectful discussion of sensitive topics.
ISBN: 0-7879-4277-4

TL76   **The Impact of Technology on Faculty Development, Life, and Work**
Kay Herr Gillespie
Describes ways to enhance faculty members' technological literacy, suggests an approach to instructional design that incorporates the possibilities of today's technologies, and examines how the online community offers an expansion of professional relationships and activities.
ISBN: 0-7879-4280-4

TL75   **Classroom Assessment and Research: An Update on Uses, Approaches, and Research Findings**
Thomas Angelo
Illustrates how classroom assessment techniques (CATs) enhance both student learning and the scholarship of teaching. Demonstrates how CATs can promote good teamwork in students, help institutions answer the call for program accountability, and guide new teachers in developing their teaching philosophies.
ISBN: 0-7879-9885-0

disciplines, including medicine, business, education, engineering, mathematics, and the sciences.
ISBN: 0-7879-9934-2

TL67   **Using Active Learning in College Classes: A Range of Options for Faculty**
Tracey E. Sutherland, Charles C. Bonwell
Examines the use of active learning in higher education and describes the concept of the active learning continuum, tying various practical examples of active learning to that concept.
ISBN: 0-7879-9933-4

TL66   **Ethical Dimensions of College and University Teaching: Understanding and Honoring the Special Relationship Between Teachers and Students**
Linc Fisch
Illustrates that responsibility to students is directly related to the understanding of one's ethical self, and that the first step in establishing that ethical identity is self-reflection. Details the transformation of structures and attitudes that ethical teaching fosters.
ISBN: 0-7879-9910-5

TL65   **Honoring Exemplary Teaching**
Marilla D. Svinicki, Robert J. Menges
Describes programs for faculty recognition in a variety of settings and with varying purposes. Reviews research relevant to selection criteria, and offers guidelines for planning and implementing effective programs.
ISBN: 0-7879-9979-2

TL64   **Disciplinary Differences in Teaching and Learning: Implications for Practice**
Nira Hativa, Michele Marincovich
Discusses causes and consequences of disciplinary differences in the patterns of teaching and learning; in the instructional strategies to increase teaching effectiveness; in the culture and environment in which teaching takes place; and in faculty and students' attitudes, goals, beliefs, values, philosophies, and orientations toward instruction.
ISBN: 0-7879-9909-1

TL63   **Understanding Self-Regulated Learning**
Paul R. Pintrich
Provides a sampling of the central issues regarding self-regulated learning in college courses and classrooms, including its definition and improving students' skills in self-regulated learning.
ISBN: 0-7879-9978-4

TL59   **Collaborative Learning: Underlying Processes and Effective Techniques**
Kris Bosworth, Sharon J. Hamilton
Provides case studies from three universities demonstrating collaborative learning in action, its potential, and its challenges. Offers guidance to faculty who wish to establish effective collaborative learning classrooms.
ISBN: 0-7879-9998-9